Student's Book

Pathway to Science 2

CB078483

Glue your picture here.

Name

Richmond

arch Skills

Example

While playing with different types of beans, the children observe that they have different shapes and colors, they are all hard to the touch, and they make a noise when they fall on the table.

The children look for a bottle cap to put the beans inside. Before they try, they ask, “How many beans will fit in the cap?”

The children answered:

- 8 beans.
- The number of beans depends on the type of bean.

What Do I Need?

- a bottle cap
- black and white beans

What Do I Do?

1. Place the bottle cap on the table.
2. Put the black beans in one at a time, until it is full.
3. Count the beans in the cap.
4. Now do the same using the white beans.

The children recorded their results in a table:

	White Beans	Black Beans
Number of Beans	9	13

When the experiment was done for a second time, the number of beans changed.

The number of beans changed because the beans are different sizes.

Richmond
58 St Aldates
Oxford
OX1 1ST
United Kingdom

Pathway to Science Student's Book Level 2

First Edition: 2014
Twenty-third Reprint: February 2022
ISBN: 978-607-06-0905-3

Pathway to Science 2 is a collaborative work, created and designed by the Department of Educational Research of Santillana.
© Richmond Publishing, S.A. de C.V. 2014
Av. Río Mixcoac No. 274, Col. Acacias,
Benito Juárez, C.P. 03240, Ciudad de México

Publisher: Justine Piekarowicz
Editor: Dominic Wright
Art and Design Coordinator: Marisela Pérez
Pre-Press Coordinator: Daniel Santillán

Illustrations: Álvaro de la Vega Arancibia, Digital Stuff

Photographs: César Vargas Ulloa
©REPOSITORIO: Grupo Santillana; © THINKSTOCK: Creatas p. 138 (Creatas Images); iStock pp. 24 (Jerry Carpenter), 25 (nattanan726), 40 (zhuzhu), 54 (Wesley Jenkins), 55 (NaluPhoto, Leroy Julien, Edson Grandisoli), 56 (christopher smith), 58 (pigphoto), 111 (Stefan Ekernas, Chee-Onn Leong), 123 (Dmitry Vasilyev), 124 (mouse_sonya), 125 (Glenn Nagel), 134 (olliemtdog, AndreaWillmore), 135 (Mitja Mladkovic), 136 (vetas), 137 (macro_jarek), (Jacek Chabraszewski); Photos.com pp. 55 (Hemera Technologies), 137 (Jupiterimages); Stockbyte pp. 40 (Comstock), 72 (Jupiterimages), 128 (altrendo images), 137 (Stockbyte); TongRo Images p. 134 (TongRo Images); Zoonar p. 55 (Zoonar RF); p. 26 (Ingram Publishing), 55 (Purestock)
2005 bazzat2003 p. 12, *Tachyglossus aculeatus*
2005 Kevin Walsh p. 16, Eggs of the Nile crocodile
Dr. Philip Bethge p. 12, *Platypus Ornithorhynchus anatinus*
Cover Design: Erika Martínez
Cover Photograph: iStock (Reto Kunz), Soft coral polyps / Octocoral

All rights reserved. No part of this work may be reproduced, stored in a retrieval system or transmitted in any form or by any means without prior written permission from the Publisher.

Richmond publications may contain links to third party websites or apps. We have no control over the content of these websites or apps, which may change frequently, and we are not responsible for the content or the way it may be used with our materials. Teachers and students are advised to exercise discretion when accessing the links.

The Publisher has made every effort to trace the owner of copyrighted material; however, the Publisher will correct any involuntary omission at the earliest opportunity.

First published by Santillana del Pacífico S.A. de Ediciones

Printed in Brazil by Forma Certa Gráfica Digital
Lote: 808132
Codigo: 292709053 / 2025

Scientific Res

Process	
Observe and Question	**Observation** You use your five senses to **observe** the world around you. You use your eyes, nose, skin, mouth, and ears.
	Research Questions If you **observe** and then ask a question, **you are formulating a research question**. How…?, What…? and How much…? are **question** words that can help you form a good research question.
	Predictions When you think of a **possible answer** to your research question, that is a **prediction**.
Plan and Conduct Research	**The Basic Framework** If you want to check or prove your predictions, you need to explore and experiment. • First, you collect the **supplies** you need for your experiment. • Then you follow the **steps**. This will help you answer your research question. • When experimenting, you use **instruments** and **measurements**.
	Results When you **draw** or **write** down your observations, you are **recording** your results.
Analyze Evidence and Communicate	**Analyze** When you look for **similarities** or **differences** in your results, you are **analyzing**.
	Conclusion When you **compare** your analysis to your results, you can make a **conclusion**. This will answer your research question.

To discover the world around us we use our...

Scientific Research Skills

Introduction

Hi friends!

We are **Spot**  and **Kiki** , and we are here to welcome you to **Pathway to Science**. Follow this pathway to a very special place. Do you want to know why it is so special?

- It is full of magic, and everyone is welcome in it. You will find information, texts, pictures and activities presented in a simple and friendly manner. Here you will discover that learning is fun!
- This is a space where we can all learn to share and live together. The activities will help us reflect on our values and learn to respect others.
- It is open to people from all over the world, a place where you can continue to learn more and interactively with the help of the latest technology.
- It is filled with adventures, challenges and experiences that will help you understand the world around you, take care of yourself and respect the environment.

We will be with you every step of the way!
All you need is curiosity and the desire to learn.

How is your textbook organized?

Pathway to Science 2 is organized into five units. Here is what you will find in each unit.

Initial Pages

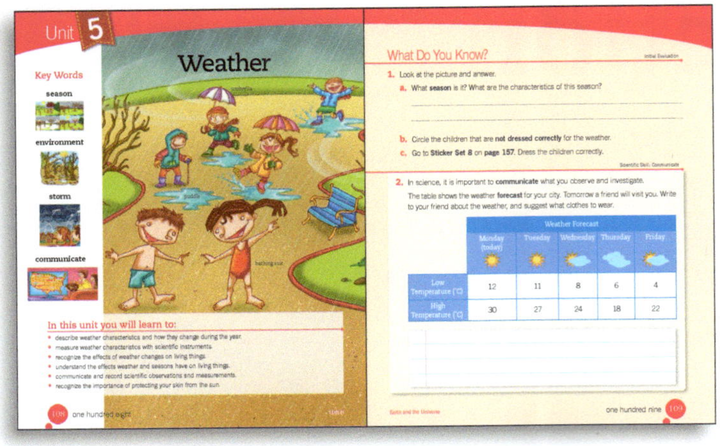

- Number and title of the unit
- Learning objectives
- Initial evaluation

Organized into Sections

- Let's Connect
  Observe, read, explore and answer.
- Let's Practice
- Let's Summarize
- Quiz Yourself

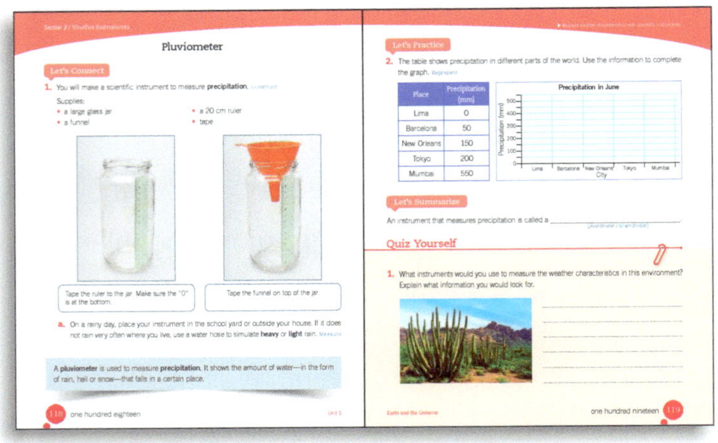

Fun Features

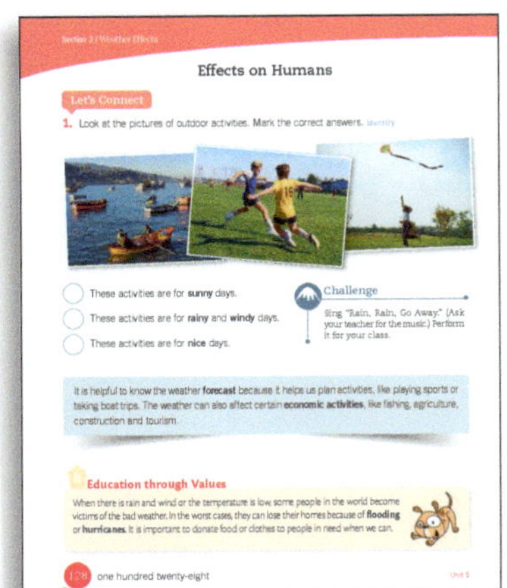

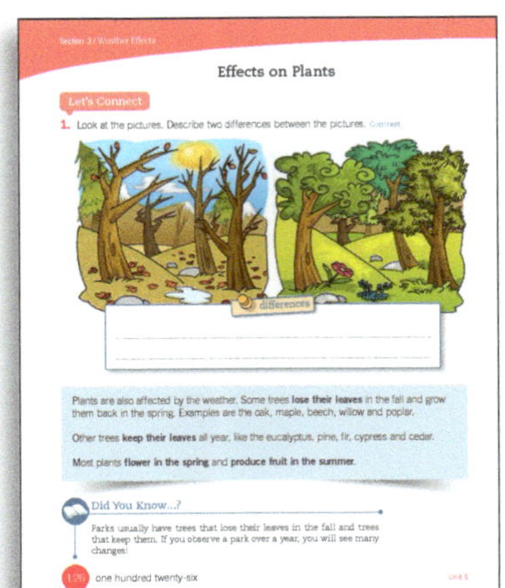

- Education through Values
- Staying Healthy
- Did You Know...?
- Remember
- Tip
- Word Focus
- Fun Fact!
- Challenge

Evaluation Pages

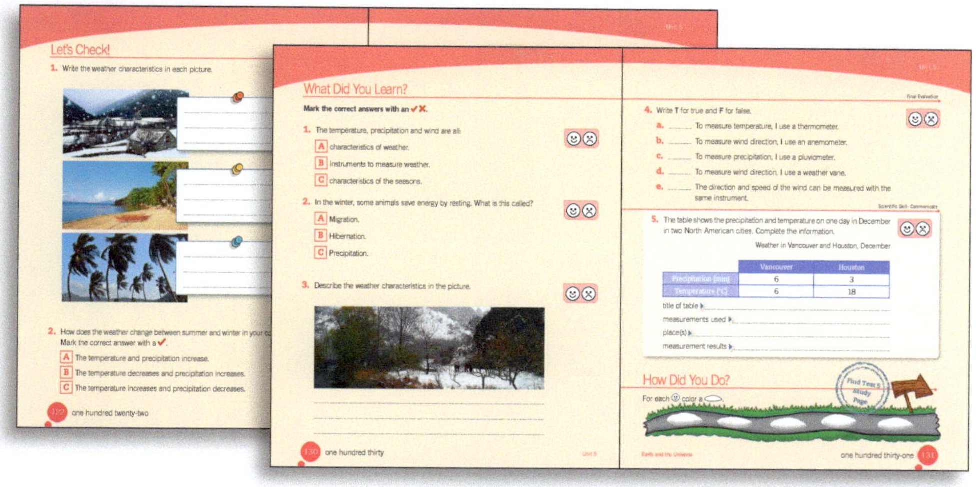

- What Do You Know?
  Initial Evaluation
- Let's Check!
  Intermediate Evaluation
- What Did You Learn?
  Final Evaluation

Special Pages

- Science Lab
- Test Study Pages
  Summary and Review

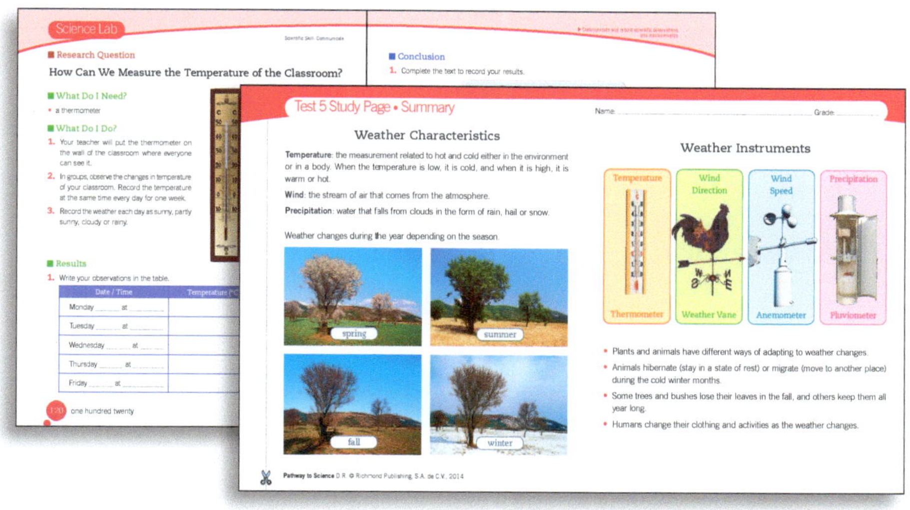

Support Pages

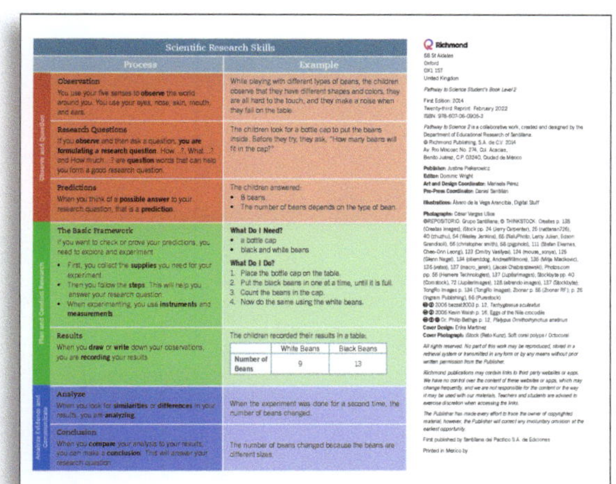

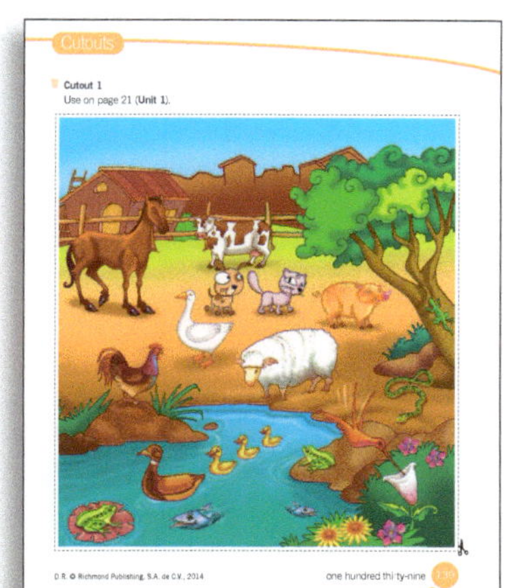

- Scientific Method Foldout
- Invertebrate Album
- Cutouts
- Stickers
- Activity Cards

Table of Contents

Unit 1

Animals

Key Words

habitat

respect

womb

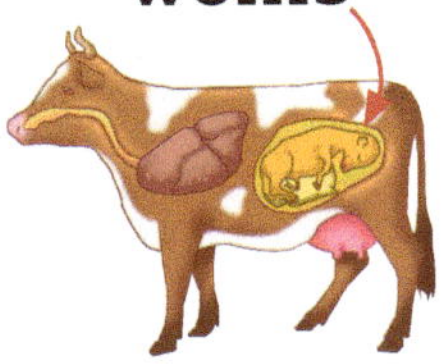

hatch

move

In this unit you will learn to:

- characterize vertebrates: mammals and birds.
- characterize vertebrates: reptiles, amphibians and fish.
- characterize invertebrates and compare them with vertebrates.
- compare the life cycles of different animals.
- predict invertebrate behavior.
- value the importance of respecting all animals.

What Do You Know?

Initial Evaluation

1. Look at the animals in the picture. Circle.

- have **hair**
- hatch from **eggs**
- develop in their **mother's womb**
- have **scales**
- **fly**

2. Why are the animals in the picture considered living things? Mark with a ✓.

They breathe. ◯ They are alive. ◯ They eat. ◯ They grow. ◯

Scientific Skill: Predict

3. Let's work like scientists! It is very important for scientists to imagine what will happen when they do research. This is called a prediction.

   a. Look at the picture. Draw a line from the chicken to the object it will walk to.

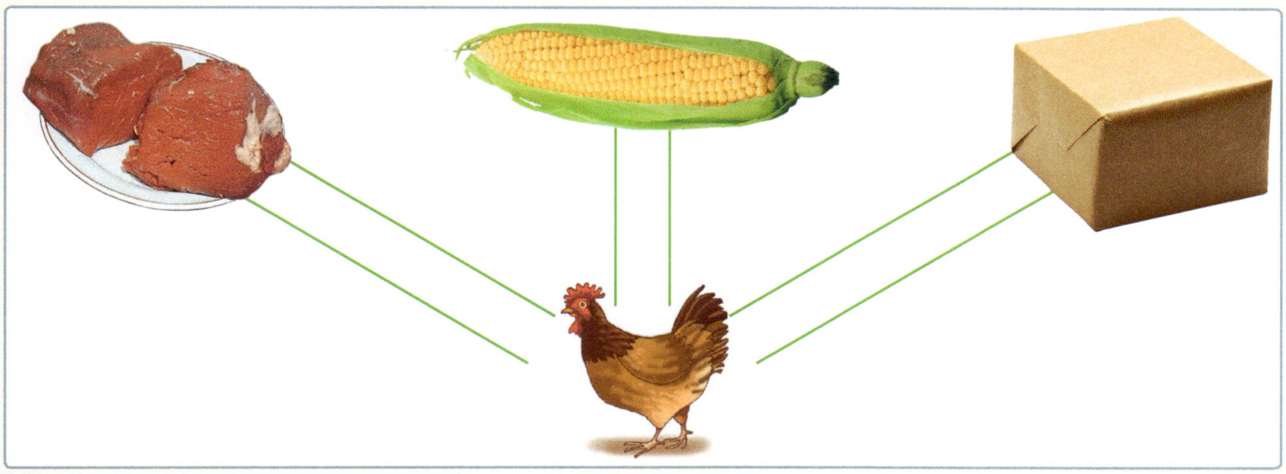

   b. Why do you think it will go there?

   ____

Vertebrate Characteristics

Let's Connect

1. For this activity you will need a pencil and some clay. After the activity, answer the questions. Interpret

- Make eight little balls of clay (the size of a ping-pong ball).
- Make two towers of four balls. Look at the picture.
- Push the pencil through the middle of one of the towers.
- Now look at the towers. What do you see?

Be careful when you push in the pencil. Don't hurt yourself!

a. Which tower is more stable?

____

b. Why is one of the towers more stable? What does the pencil do?

____

Some animals have **bones** in their bodies. These bones form an **internal skeleton**. A skeleton gives the body shape and strength, just like the pencil did for the tower. Animals that have a skeleton are called **vertebrates**; those that do not are called **invertebrates**. There are five types of vertebrates: **mammals**, **birds**, **reptiles**, **amphibians** and **fish**. Their bodies consist of three parts: the **head**, **torso** and **limbs**. Many vertebrates also have **tails**.

Let's Practice

2. Match the animals with the correct **groups**. Relate

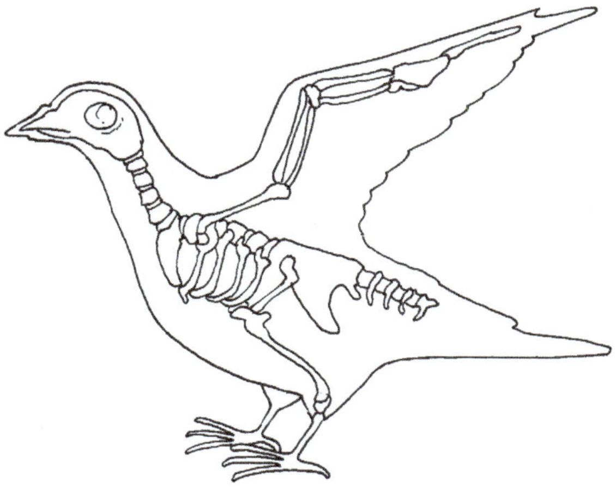

vertebrates

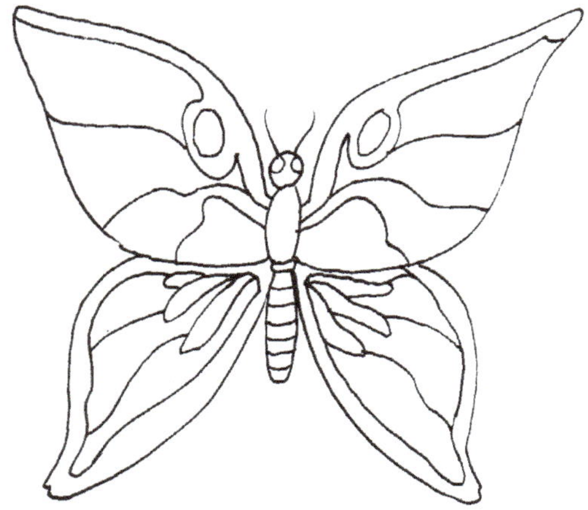

invertebrates

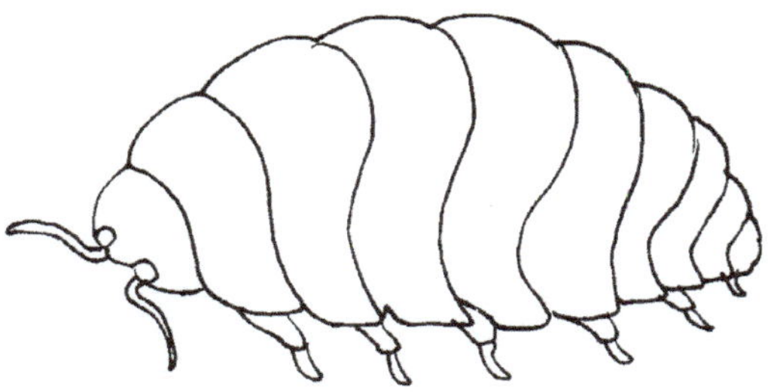

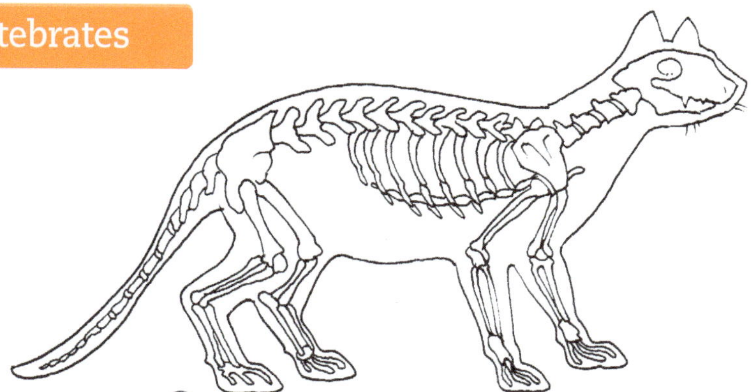

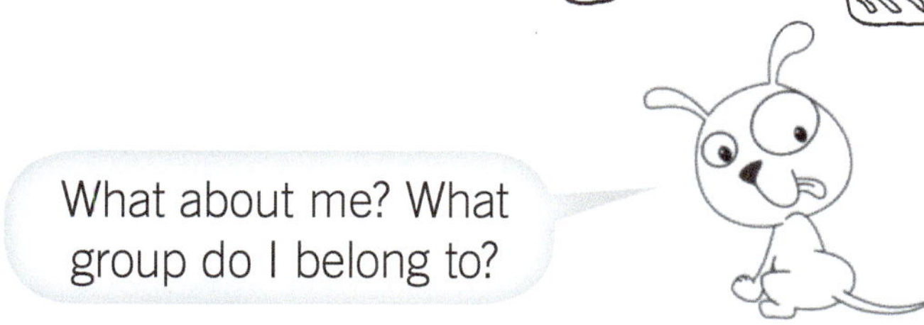

a. Circle the animals with the most fragile bodies.

3. Color the different **body parts** of the animals. Characterize

Let's Summarize

Animals that have a skeleton are called **vertebrates**. Animals that do not have a **skeleton** are called **invertebrates**.

Mammals

Let's Connect

1. Read the information about mammals. Explain

Mammals eat different food when they are adults. Their teeth are different because of what they need to eat.

Parents care for their babies. **Offspring** drink their mother's **milk**.

Most mammals are **viviparous** animals: babies grow inside the female before they are born. The exceptions are the echidna and the duck-billed platypus, which are both oviparous. They are the only two egg-laying mammals on earth!

Their bodies stay the same temperature, they are warm-blooded, and they **breathe** with their **lungs**.

Their bodies are covered in **hair**.

Most mammals are **terrestrial**. Some are **aquatic**, like whales and dolphins, or **aerial-terrestrial,** like bats.

They have four **limbs,** which are usually legs. Mammals can also have two feet and two wings, or fins.

Challenge

Draw a picture of yourself on a blank sheet of paper. Next, label your body parts. Now label three things that make you a mammal. Which ones did you choose?

Let's Practice

2. Read about dolphins and answer. Infer

Dolphins are mammals that live in water. They are excellent divers, but they have **lungs** like humans, so they need to swim to the surface to breathe.

a. Which place is a better home for a dolphin? Mark the correct answer.

b. Why do dolphins **not** have feet? Hint: Think about their habitat.

____

____

3. Write **T** for true and **F** for false. Differentiate

a. ☐ Mammals are covered in scales.

b. ☐ Mammals are vertebrates.

c. ☐ All mammals are viviparous.

d. ☐ Mammal offspring drink their mother's milk.

Word Focus

Offspring is the word we use for the young of animals. You can use it for humans, too!

Let's Summarize

Mammals are animals that drink their mother's milk after birth. They have hair on their bodies and they breathe with their lungs.

Birds

Let's Connect

1. Look and read about the characteristics of birds. Identify

a. In which habitats—air, land or water—can birds move?

____

Education through Values

Many birds make their nests in trees. Look at the picture. What the boy is doing is very bad for the birds. Now the eggs will not develop or hatch into baby birds.

Remember to respect all living things on earth. We are all important.

Let's Practice

2. Find the characteristics of birds. Mark with a ✔. Identify

◯ Oviparous.	◯ Viviparous.	◯ Most fly.	◯ They have feet.
◯ They have wings.	◯ They have hair.	◯ They have lungs.	◯ They have feathers.

Let's Summarize

Birds are **vertebrates**. They are covered in feathers, are oviparous and breathe with their lungs. Most birds can fly.

Quiz Yourself

1. Look at the photographs. Mark the characteristics of each animal. Write the names of the groups.

	 orangutan	 dog	 toucan
Has lungs			
Has feathers			
Is oviparous			
Drinks milk			
Animal group			

Section
2 More Vertebrates

Reptiles

Let's Connect

1. Look at the photographs. Answer the questions. Describe

sea turtle

snake

crocodile

a. Focus on the animal's skin. How are the vertebrates similar?

b. How does each vertebrate move? Do they use the same body parts?

The animals in the photographs are **reptiles.** Most reptiles live on land, but some are **aquatic**. Reptiles have skin covered in **scales**. They are **oviparous** and breathe with their **lungs**. Reptiles that live in water have to come to the surface to breathe.

Did You Know...?

Most reptiles lay their eggs in the ground. The outside of the egg is very thick and keeps the inside humid.

Challenge

Move like a snake, a crocodile and a turtle. Race your friends!

Let's Practice

2. Color the body part that each reptile uses to move. Identify

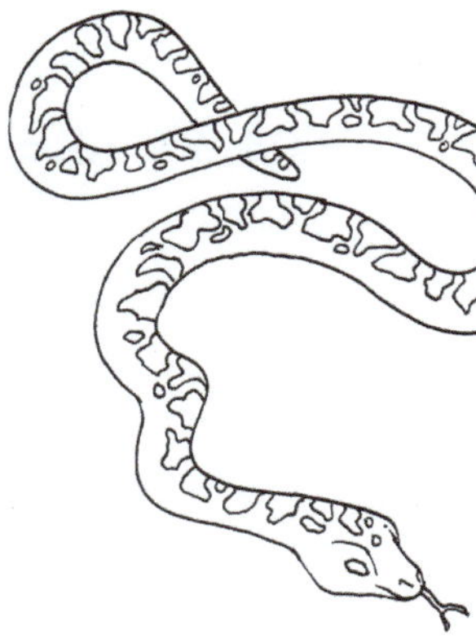
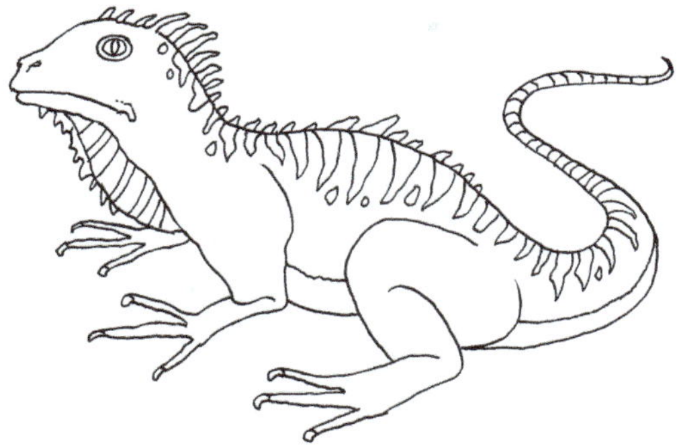

3. Why can none of these reptiles live in a closed fish tank? Think about how each one breathes and reproduces. Answer. Apply

Respiration: ______________________________

____

____

Reproduction: ______________________________

____

____

Word Focus

Respiration is the action of breathing.

Tip

Sentence starter:
- These reptiles cannot live in a closed space because they…

Let's Summarize

Reptiles are vertebrates that hatch from eggs, breathe with their lungs and have skin covered in scales.

Some people have iguanas as pets. They take care of them just like a cat or dog, without knowing what they really need. What do you think about that?

Amphibians and Fish

Let's Connect

1. Look at the photographs of the amphibians and fish. Match the vertebrates with the correct characteristics. Associate

Their skin is covered in **scales**. ◯

They always stay in water. ◯

They have **fins**. ◯

They hatch from **eggs**. ◯

They live on land and in water. ◯

They have hairless, wet and thin skin. ◯

They always breathe through **gills**. ◯

As adults they breathe air with their lungs ◯

Most hatch from eggs. Some, like sharks and seahorses, are viviparous. ◯

They have feet to move. ◯

a. Color (green) the shared characteristics of fish and amphibians.

b. Color (orange) the characteristics they do not share.

Fun Fact!

Gills are like lungs on the outside of the body. Fish and amphibians use them to breathe.

Let's Practice

2. Go to **Sticker Set 1** on **page 151**. Stick the skin of each animal in the correct circle. Identify

3. Complete the chart with the characteristics of amphibians and fish. Describe

		Amphibians	Fish
a.	What organs do they use to breathe?		
b.	How do they reproduce?		
c.	Where do they live?		

Let's Summarize

Fish live in water. They have skin covered in scales, and they breathe through gills. Amphibians breathe through gills only when they are babies. As adults they breathe with lungs. They have hairless skin and live both in water and on land. Most fish and all amphibians lay eggs to reproduce.

Comparing Vertebrates

Let's Connect

1. Look at the chart. Answer the questions. Analyze

Groups of Vertebrates

	Mammals	Birds	Reptiles	Amphibians	Fish

Body Covering	hair	feathers	scales	hairless	scales
Respiration	lungs	lungs	lungs	gills and lungs	gills
Reproduction	viviparous	oviparous	oviparous	oviparous	oviparous
Habitat	land and water	land, air and water	land and water	land and water	water

a. Human beings are also vertebrates. Which group do we belong to?

____

b. Which vertebrates **have similar** body coverings?

____

c. Which vertebrates **are different** because of their respiration and reproduction?

____

Let's Practice

2. Go to **Cutout 1** on **page 139**. Circle the vertebrates with the correct color. Glue the cutout in your notebook. Identify

- mammals
- birds
- reptiles
- amphibians
- fish

Let's Summarize

Vertebrates can be mammals, birds, reptiles, amphibians or fish. Each group has its own characteristics.

Quiz Yourself

1. Match each description with the correct group of vertebrates.

I have hair and I breathe with my lungs.	amphibians
I have feathers and I lay eggs.	mammals
I have scales and I breathe through gills.	fish
I have scales and I breathe with my lungs.	birds
I have hairless skin and I lay eggs.	reptiles

Let's Check!

1. Look at the picture. Write the **missing** words.

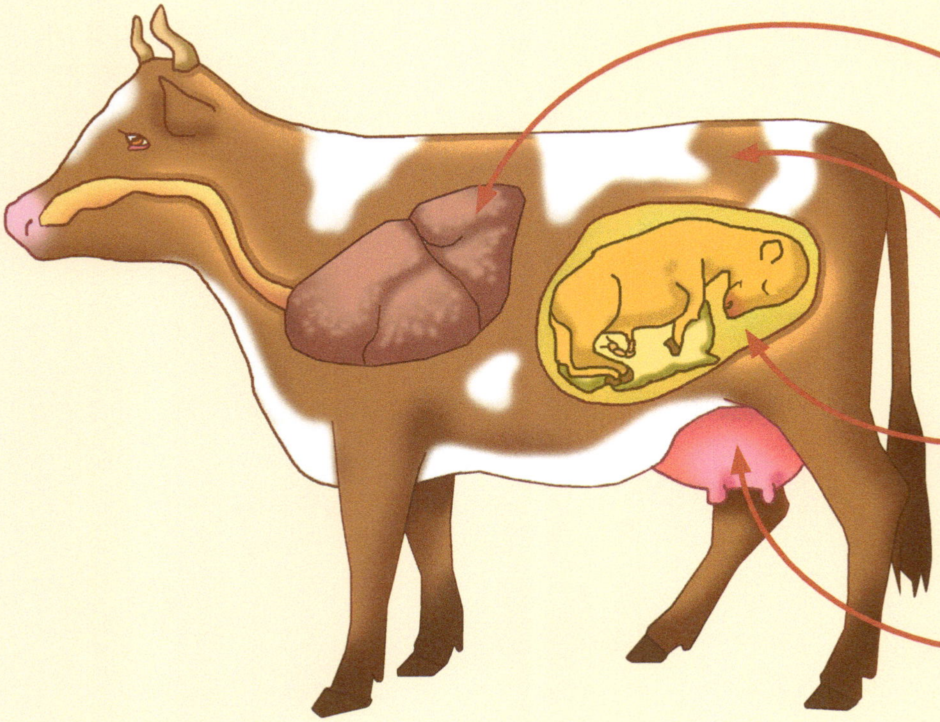

a. It breathes with ______________________.

b. Its skin is covered in ______________________.

c. Its reproduction is ______________________.

d. Its offspring drinks ______________________.

2. Match each vertebrate group with the correct characteristics. Each group has more than one characteristic.

oviparous	amphibians		lungs
viviparous	birds		land
gills	fish		scales
	mammals		
	reptiles		
hair	feathers	air	water

3. Find and circle the six animals in the word search. Write five of their names under the correct groups.

☺ ☹

S	W	E	Z	H	P	E	N	G	U	I	N
A	X	K	E	I	D	N	Q	V	A	C	A
L	O	P	B	J	F	O	Z	B	R	T	F
M	L	Y	R	T	G	R	C	N	K	Y	R
O	Q	Z	A	M	S	N	A	K	E	W	O
N	F	B	U	T	T	E	R	F	L	Y	G

birds ______________

mammals ______________

reptiles ______________

amphibians ______________

fish ______________

a. Which animal is an invertebrate? ______________________________

How Did You Do?

For each ☺ color a ⬭.

Invertebrate Characteristics

Let's Connect

1. Read the information about invertebrates. What do you observe? Explain

Some have no limbs, some have legs, and others have wings.

They can be aquatic, terrestrial, aerial or a combination.

Invertebrates can be carnivores, herbivores or omnivores.

All are oviparous.

Invertebrates do not have an internal skeleton. Sometimes, a hard outer shell covers their bodies.

A lot of invertebrates are insects. Insect bodies are divided into a head, a thorax and an abdomen. They also have legs.

Did You Know...?

Grasshoppers "chirp" by rubbing their back legs together. They also use their big back legs to jump.

Fun Fact!

In the movies *A Bug's Life* and *Ants*, you can observe some characteristics and behaviors of invertebrates.

Let's Practice

2. Complete the information card for each animal. Mark the correct characteristics with a ✔. Identify

Spider

Type of animal:	◯ invertebrate		◯ vertebrate
Habitat:	◯ land		◯ water
Reproduction:	◯ eggs		◯ womb
Limbs:	◯ legs	◯ wings	◯ none

Butterfly

Type of animal:	◯ invertebrate		◯ vertebrate
Habitat:	◯ air and land		◯ water
Reproduction:	◯ eggs		◯ womb
Limbs:	◯ legs	◯ wings	◯ none

3. Write the name of each part of this insect's body. Identify

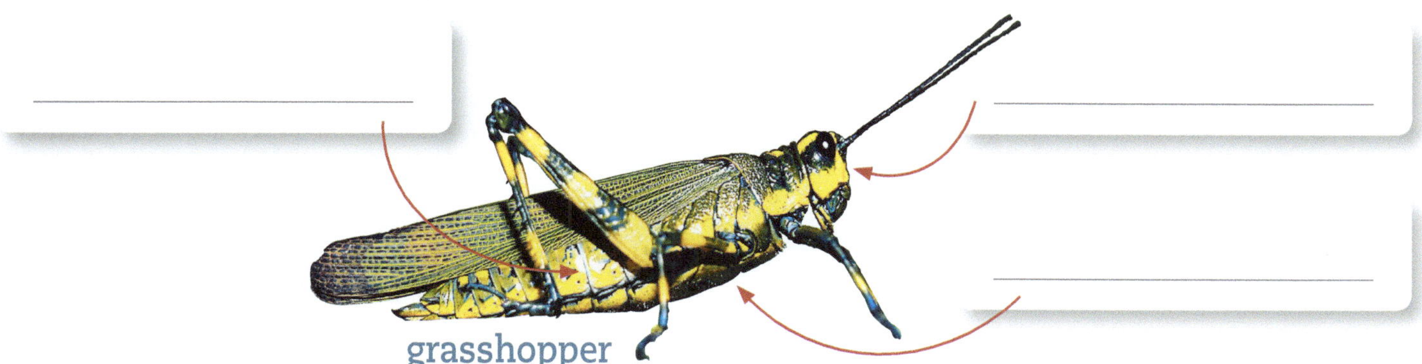

grasshopper

Let's Summarize

Invertebrates do not have a skeleton inside their bodies. They lay eggs to reproduce. Also, some have wings and antennae, and some have shells.

Groups of Invertebrates

Let's Connect

1. Invertebrates are classified into groups by their characteristics. Read and answer the questions. Infer

Arthropods

These are the largest group of invertebrates found in nature. In this group, there are three main types:

Insects

These have two antennae, six legs and usually four wings.

Arachnids

These have eight legs and do not have antennae or wings.

Crustaceans

These have two pairs of antennae and ten legs. A shell covers the thorax of many crustaceans. Most live in water.

Complete the **Invertebrate Album** on **page 132.** There you will learn about other groups of invertebrates in nature.

a. How many legs do arthropods have?

____

b. How do crustaceans protect their bodies?

____

Tip

Sentence starters:
- Arthropods have...
- Crustaceans have a...

Let's Practice

2. The pictures below show some arthropods. Color the insects (orange), the arachnids (green) and the crustaceans (blue). Classify

bee

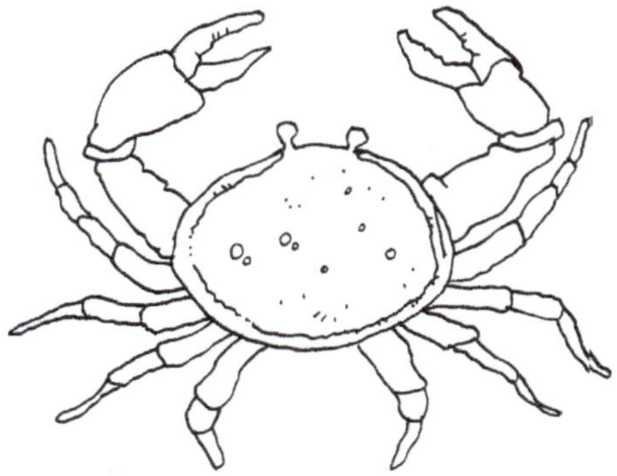
crab

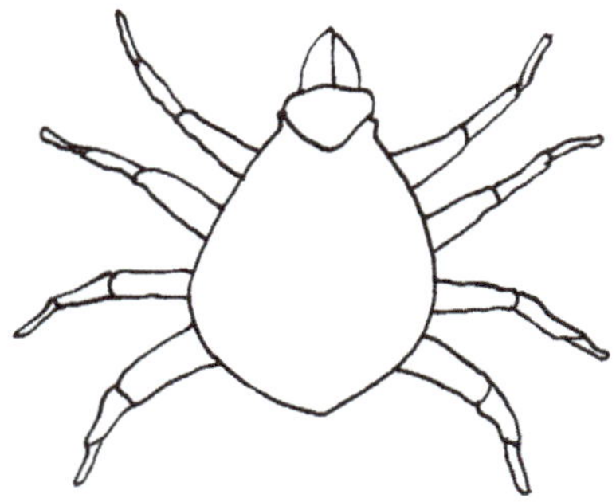
tick

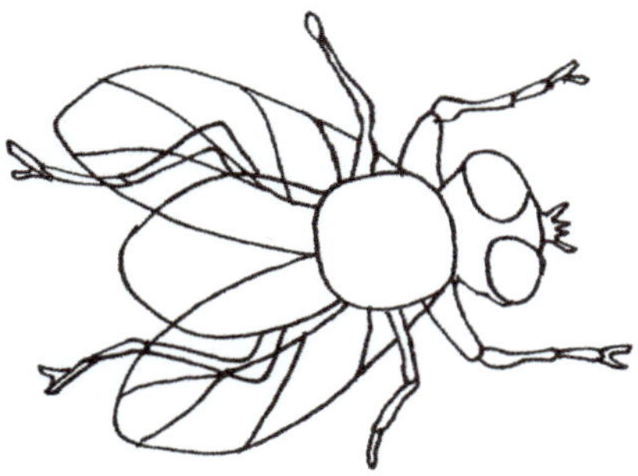
fly

lobster

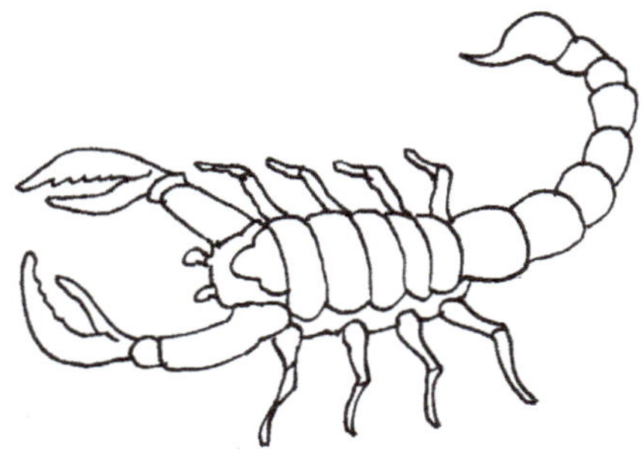
scorpion

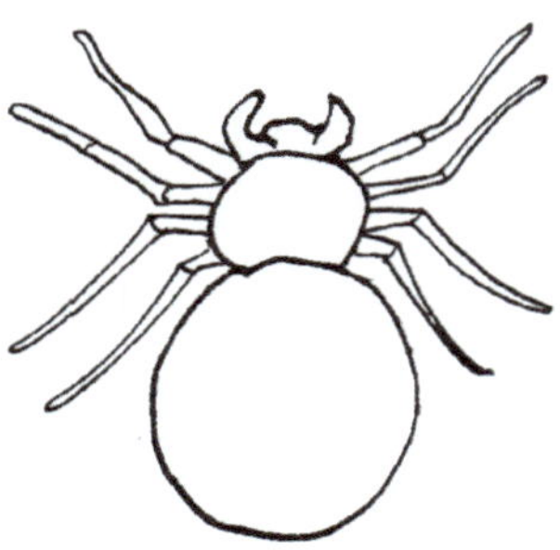
spider

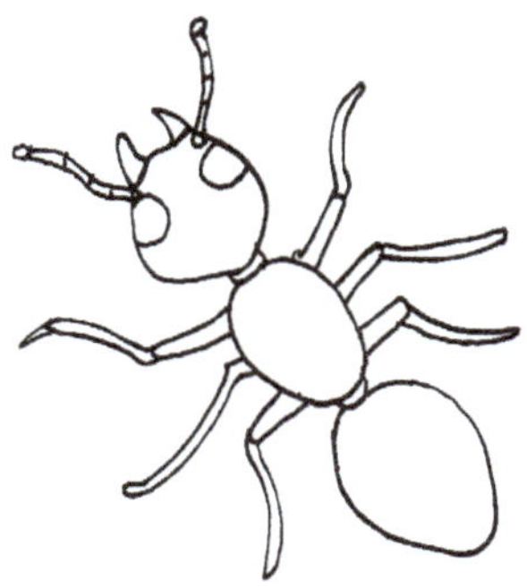
ant

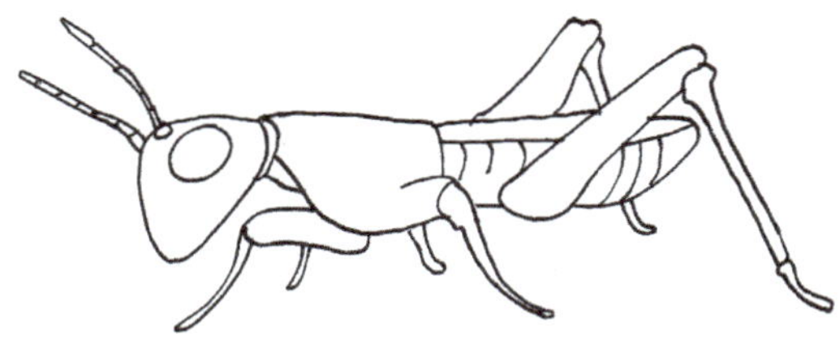
grasshopper

Let's Summarize

Invertebrates are classified into different groups. The largest group is arthropods, which includes insects, arachnids and crustaceans.

Comparing Vertebrates and Invertebrates

Let's Connect

1. Look at the photographs. Answer the questions. Compare and contrast

condor

moth

a. What makes these two animals similar? ______________________

b. What makes them different? ______________________

c. Which of these animals is a vertebrate? ______________________

d. Which is an invertebrate? ______________________

When comparing vertebrates with invertebrates, remember that vertebrates have an internal skeleton. It supports their bodies and helps them move. Invertebrates do not have a skeleton. Both vertebrates and invertebrates live on land or in water, and some fly.

Let's Practice

2. Mark the correct group for each animal with a ✔. Classify

Vertebrate				
Invertebrate				

Let's Summarize

Vertebrates have an internal skeleton. Invertebrates do not. This is the main difference between vertebrates and invertebrates.

Quiz Yourself

1. How many vertebrates are there in the picture? ☐ vertebrates.

- Circle:
  - invertebrates that fly
  - vertebrates that fly
  - animals with eight legs
  - arthropods

Research Question

Where Will the Ants Go?

What Do I Need?

- 1 spoonful of sugar
- a clear plastic container with a lid
- soil

To observe is to find information about something using **all five senses.** **Remember to be careful!** Always ask your teacher before you touch, smell or taste anything.

To predict is to imagine a possible answer. Use what you know and try to guess the result of the experiment before you start.

What Do I Do?

1. Look for ants and carefully collect them. Then put some soil and the ants in the plastic container.
2. **Observe** how the ants move. You can use a magnifying glass.
3. If you put sugar in the container, where do you think the ants will go? Go to **Sticker Set 2** on **page 151**. Stick the ants where you think they will go.

When you stick the ants on the picture and talk about what will happen, you are **predicting!**

4. Now put a spoonful of sugar in the container. Observe where the ants go. Are they moving in the same direction as before?
5. Once you have finished the activity, put the ants back where you found them.

Results

1. When you put sugar in the container, did your prediction come true? Did the ants go where you thought they would go? Explain.

____

____

2. If you replace the sugar with honey, do you think the same thing will happen? Explain.

____

____

3. What do you predict will happen if you add flour instead of sugar or honey?

____

____

Conclusion

4. Why do you think the ants moved toward the sugar?

____

____

Why is it important to put the ants back in their natural habitat after the experiment?

In this science lab, you **observed** a situation and **predicted** what would happen. In other words, you imagined an answer before knowing the result. Have you done this before? When?

Animal Life Cycles

Stages of Life

Let's Connect

Living things go through a series of changes in their lives: **they are born**, **they grow**, **they reproduce**, and **they die**. All these changes are part of the **life cycle**. Animals also experience changes during **development**.

1. Look at the development of the following animals. Discuss. Infer

Some characteristics of animals change during their growth and **development**. Other things stay the same.

Some animals go through very big body changes as they grow. This process is called **metamorphosis**.

a. Is human development similar to the pictures? Why or why not?

b. Do you think mammal development is called **metamorphosis**?

Let's Practice

2. Look at the life cycle of a frog. Number the stages from 1 to 5. Sequence

◯ Its tail gets smaller, and the frog keeps growing until it is an adult.

◯ Adult frogs lay many eggs.

◯ Baby frogs are called tadpoles. They hatch from eggs, breathe through gills and grow as they eat algae and other aquatic plants.

◯ Metamorphosis starts when a tadpole starts to grow legs.

◯ When the legs are fully formed and the gills change to lungs, the young frog begins to breathe and it moves to land.

3. Frogs develop in which two habitats? Characterize

____

Go to **Activity Cards 1** and **2**, and play with your classmates!

Let's Summarize

Living things go through different stages: they are born, they grow, they reproduce, and they die. All these changes are part of the life cycle. Some animals go through big changes, called **metamorphosis**.

Life Cycles in Different Habitats

Let's Connect

1. Some animal life cycles have stages that happen in different places, like the life cycle of the frog. Go to **Cutout 2** on **page 141**. Glue the cutouts in the correct order in the life cycles. Mark the animals that grow in more than one habitat. Sequence

dog ◯

spider ◯

sea turtle ◯

a. In your notebook, draw the missing stages of life for each animal. Illustrate

Let's Practice

2. Answer the questions about each animal's life cycle. Use the frog as an example.
Compare and contrast

	Does it go through metamorphosis?	Does it stay in one habitat while it develops?	In which habitat(s) does it live?
Frog	yes	no	water and land
Dog			
Butterfly			
Chicken			
Sea Turtle			
Spider			

Let's Summarize

Life cycles of some animals have stages that happen in different places.

Quiz Yourself

1. Go to **Sticker Set 3** on **page 151.** Put a fly's life cycle in the correct order.

a. Does the fly go through metamorphosis? ☐ yes ☐ no

b. Do all the stages of its life happen in the same habitat? ☐ yes ☐ no

What Did You Learn?

1. Complete the crossword puzzle using the clues.

a. Animals **without** bones.

b. Animals with scales and lungs.

c. Animals that are born from living things and drink their mother's milk.

d. All the changes from birth to death in all living things.

e. Animals with scales and gills.

2. Which group of vertebrates is oviparous and has feathers? Mark the correct answer with a ✔.

A Birds.

B Reptiles.

C Amphibians.

3. The development stages of the salmon are out of order. Number them in order from 1 to 5.

4. What happens if amphibian eggs are on dry land? Mark the correct answer.

- They dry up, and the tadpoles live.
- They stay wet, and the tadpoles live.
- They dry up, and the tadpoles die.

How Did You Do?

For each ☺ color a ⬭.

Unit 2

Wild Animals

Key Words

clean

shelter

garbage

hunt

at risk

In this unit you will learn to:

- compare the characteristics of different habitats.
- communicate the effects humans have on the environment.
- identify animals at risk of extinction and propose ways to protect them.
- experiment with animal habitat characteristics.
- recognize the importance of recycling and taking care of nature.

What Do You Know?

Initial Evaluation

1. Go to **Sticker Set 4** on **page 153**. Stick the animals in the correct habitats.

2. Write the number of animals in each habitat.

☐ aquatic ☐ terrestrial

☐ aerial and terrestrial ☐ aquatic and terrestrial

Scientific Skill: Experiment

3. Ralph took an animal from the ocean. The animal is **marked** in the picture. He wants to know where the animal will be the most comfortable.

When he gets home, he fills three **aquariums** with water. Then he:

- Adds sugar to the first aquarium.
- Adds salt to the second aquarium.
- Does not add anything to the third aquarium.

Ralph put the **starfish** in each aquarium. By doing this, Ralph can see that the correct habitat for the animal is the aquarium with water and salt. This is the closest to its natural habitat.

a. Do you think Ralph took the best steps to find the animal's habitat? Explain.

____

____

b. What would you do?

____

____

Animal Environments

Habitats

Let's Connect

1. Look at the photographs. Answer the questions. Infer

a. Where do you think the **most** animals **live**? Mark the correct box.

☐ habitat 1　☐ habitat 2　☐ habitat 3

b. Write the correct number under each animal's name.

shark	monkey	coyote
________	________	________

The different environments of living things are called **habitats**. In its habitat, each living thing can find **food** and **shelter** to survive. Some habitats are: **forests**, **grasslands**, **rivers**, **oceans** and **deserts**. Each habitat has its own characteristics.

Did You Know...?

Your house can be a habitat for animals like the recluse spider! This spider's bite can be **fatal**, so keeping a clean house is very important.

Let's Practice

2. Help each animal **find its habitat**. Identify

3. Can any of the animals above live in **two habitats**? Explain. Analyze

____

____

Let's Summarize

A habitat is the ____________________ where a living thing develops. In its habitat, a living thing can find ____________________ and ____________________ to survive.

Education through Values

Human habitats are the houses we live in. It is very important to take care of our houses and keep them clean. It is important to keep a pet's area clean, too!

Habitats: Light or Dark

Let's Connect

1. Look at the pictures. Answer the questions. Infer

a. Why do you think you see **different animals** in the **same habitat** during the **day** and at **night**?

____

b. Find the mole in the picture. Where is its **habitat**?

____

Fun Fact!

Nocturnal animals sleep during the day. **Diurnal** animals sleep at night. Which one are you?

Challenge

Find and label the following animals: owl, snake, bat, rabbit, ant, deer and mouse.

Light is a characteristic of habitats that influences animals. Almost all animals have habitats related to light or darkness. For example, most birds are **awake** during the day and live in trees, but bats are awake at night and live in caves.
Most animals use the **ground** of their habitats to **move** and find **food**, and some even use it for **shelter**. Others, like ants, earthworms and moles, live **underground**, where there is no light.

Let's Practice

2. Go to **Cutout 4** on **page 145**. Glue the animals in the correct boxes. Identify

I sleep at night and am active during the day.	**My habitat is the forest. I am a bird, and I capture my food at night.**	**I need the sun to live. My habitat is the garden. I am a reptile.**

3. Circle the animals according to what they are doing. Remember that their habitat is underground. Identify

finding food   moving   finding shelter

▸ Representation of an ant's underground nest.

Let's Summarize

____________________ is one characteristic of habitats. Some animals are awake during the ____________________, and others are awake at ____________________.

Temperature and Humidity

Let's Connect

1. Mark the habitat where you would like to live. Answer the questions with a partner. Identify

a. Which habitat is the **hottest**?

b. Which habitat is the **coldest**?

c. Do you like **humid** or **dry** places?

Word Focus

Temperature is a measure of the quantity of **heat** in our bodies or in the environment.

Temperature and **humidity** are other important **characteristics** of habitats. Each animal develops and lives in a place where the temperature is right for it. During the winter, some animals change habitats to live in a **warmer** place. We call this migration.
Humidity is also a very important characteristic. Humidity is a measure of the **amount of water in a habitat**. Aquatic animals live in very humid places, like rivers, lakes and the ocean. Terrestrial animals live in places with less humidity.

Let's Practice

2. Match the animals with the characteristics of their habitats. Relate

lion

polar bear

giraffe

warm and dry habitat

cold and humid habitat

penguin

whale

zebra

Let's Summarize

Habitat Characteristics

light		

Quiz Yourself

1. Look at the habitats and compare. Complete the table.

Characteristic	Habitat A	Habitat B	Same?
temperature			yes / no
light			yes / no
humidity			yes / no

Research Question

Which Habitat Do Roly-Poly Bugs Prefer?

What Do I Need?

- 3 or 4 roly-poly bugs
  Transport them carefully in a box with holes. If you can't find any, look for worms, instead.
- a cardboard box
- paper towels
- a marker
- poster board
- water

What Do I Do?

1. Put the paper towel on the bottom of the cardboard box. With the marker, draw a line to divide the box into two zones. Label them 1 and 2.
2. Cover the top of zone 1 with poster board.
3. Where do you think the bugs will go? Mark which zone you think they will prefer.

☐ zone 1 (dark) ☐ zone 2 (light)

4. Put the bugs in the center of the box. Observe where they go.
5. Remove the poster board and the bugs. Put a little water in zone 1.

Word Focus

To experiment means to test and learn something about an object or event.

6. Where do you think the bugs will go? Mark which zone you think they will prefer.

☐ zone 1 (humid) ☐ zone 2 (dry)

7. Put the bugs in the center of the box. Observe where they go.

Results

1. Was your first prediction correct?

☐ yes ☐ no

2. Was your second prediction correct?

☐ yes ☐ no

Conclusion

1. What are the characteristics of this animal's natural habitat?

____

____

2. The bugs moved to certain places in the box. What does this say about their natural habitat?

____

____

You just did an **experiment!** You tested and proved which habitat the bugs preferred by changing some of the conditions and observing what happened. Did you like the experiment?

Human Impact on the Environment

Effects on Our Surroundings

Let's Connect

1. Look at the picture. Analyze

a. Which actions have a **positive impact** on the environment? Mark them with a ✔.

b. Which actions have a **negative impact** on the environment? Mark them with an ✘.

All human activity **impacts and affects** the environment and animal habitats in some way. Things like taking care of nature, planting trees, not wasting energy or water and not polluting the air all have a **positive impact** on the environment. Other things like starting forest fires, not taking care of animals and polluting the air and water all have a **negative impact** on the environment.

Let's Practice

2. Go to **Sticker Set 5** on **page 153**. Complete the chart. Communicate

Humans have an impact on the environment. It can be:

positive	negative

To avoid negative impacts, we should:

____

____

____

Let's Summarize

Write one **positive** impact and one **negative** impact that humans have on the environment. Make sure they are different from those you have already seen in the book.

____

____

Taking Care of the Environment

Let's Connect

1. Read the conversation. Answer the questions with a partner. Analyze

a. What is wrong with the playground?

b. What are the children going to do? Why? Will it work?

There are many ways to **protect the environment**. If we want to live on a cleaner and happier planet, we need to take care of the plants, animals, land, air and water.

One way to take care of the earth is to follow the **Three Rs: Reduce, Reuse** and **Recycle**.

To **reduce** is to use fewer products and waste less energy.

To **reuse** is to invent new uses for products or objects or to use them again.

To **recycle** is to make new products out of old materials.

Let's Practice

2. Read the sentences. Mark the correct word with a ✔. Apply

		Reduce	Reuse	Recycle
a.	Use fewer tissues.			
b.	Give used toys to other children.			
c.	Bring reusable bags to the supermarket.			
d.	Draw on both sides of paper.			
e.	Use wrapping paper again.			
f.	Turn off water faucets.			
g.	Buy reusable bottles.			
h.	Put paper and plastic in recycling containers so they can be made into new products.			

Let's Summarize

Make a pledge to show that you care about the earth.

I promise to help the environment. Starting today, I will ______________________

____

Signed, ______________________
(sign your name here)

Quiz Yourself

1. Go to **Activity Card 3** and color the activities that have a **positive impact** on the environment. Take it home, and hang it up so your whole family can help protect the earth.

This is the recycling symbol. It indicates products that have been or can be recycled. I like using these products!

Let's Check!

1. Circle in  the animals that do **not** belong in this habitat.

a. Describe the **real** habitats of the animals you circled. Remember to think about temperature, humidity and light.

Animal: ____________________

Habitat characteristics: ____________________

Animal: ____________________

Habitat characteristics: ____________________

Animal: ____________________

Habitat characteristics: ____________________

2. Compare the habitats of these animals.

penguin   monkey

____

____

3. Draw a ☺ if the action has a **positive impact** on the environment. Draw a ☹ if it has a negative **impact** on the environment.

How Did You Do?

For each ☺ color a ⬭.

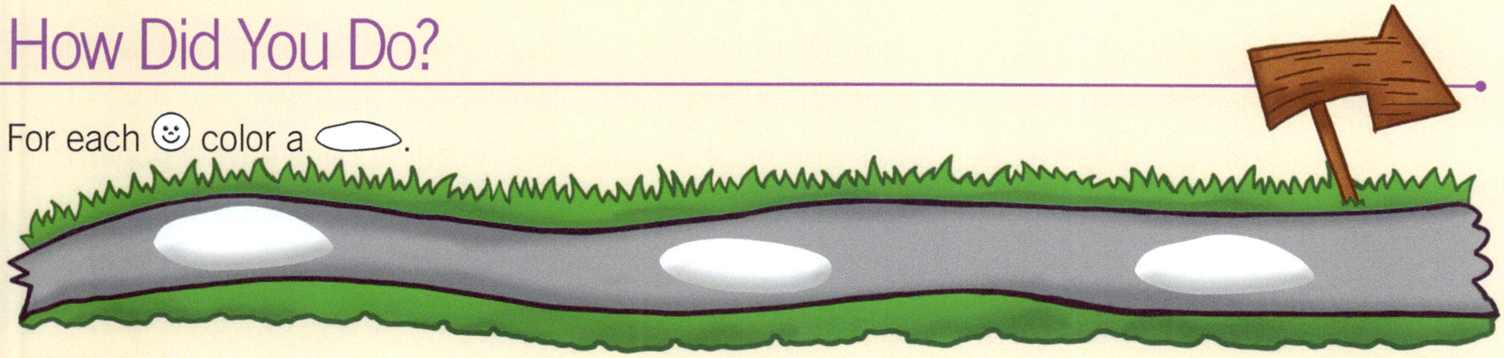

Endangered Animals

Let's Take Care of Animals

Let's Connect

1. Read the information about the animals **at risk** of extinction.

Name: Chimpanzee.

Habitat: Forests in West and Central Africa.

Food: Fruit, leaves, small mammals.

Type of Animal: Mammal.

Name: Condor.

Habitat: High mountains of the Andes and nearby grasslands.

Food: Carrion (dead animals).

Type of Animal: Bird.

a. Have you ever heard of these animals?

b. Which animals are **endangered** in your country?

c. How do you feel about people keeping rare animals as pets?

Word Focus

Endangered animals need more protection than other animals because there are **fewer** of them on earth.

Challenge

Pretend you are an endangered animal. Draw a picture of your habitat. Show how humans can help you survive.

There are some animals that can only be found in one particular country or area, such as the kangaroo in Australia and the panda in China. They are called **native animals**.
Animal habitats are **affected** by human actions. It is possible that our actions have a negative impact on the environment, causing animals to lose their habitats. If animals have no place to live, they are at **risk of extinction** and can disappear from the planet forever.

Let's Practice

2. Look at these **native animals** that are **endangered**. Match each one with its habitat. Associate

blue whale

mountains of Central Asia

manatee

Amazon

snow leopard

ocean

blue macaw

tropical river

Let's Summarize

Some human ____________ (activities / information) have a negative impact on animal ____________ (spaces / habitats).
They put some ____________ (native / common) animals at risk of extinction.

Let's Help Our Animals!

Let's Connect

1. Read the text below. Answer the questions with a classmate. Identify

Animal at Risk!

Many animals are endangered because they are **hunted** for meat, fur or feathers. Sometimes they are **captured** and sold as pets.

One example is the spider monkey. These monkeys live at the top of the tallest trees in rain forests of Central and South America. **Deforestation** is another reason they are at risk.

a. What is the name of the animal in the picture? Why is it endangered?

b. Do you know of any other endangered animals? Why are they endangered?

Word Focus

Deforestation is when all the trees in an area are cut down.

To keep animals safe, humans should **take care of animal habitats** and **stop hunting**. Some parks and reserves have been created to help protect animals. Every country has native animals that need to be protected.

Let's Practice

2. Write two more **ways to protect endangered** native animals. Follow the example. Give examples

a. Do not hunt them for any reason.

b. ______________________________

c. ______________________________

Let's Summarize

Many ______________ animals are at risk of ______________. It is important to ______________ them so they do not disappear.

Quiz Yourself

1. Look at the picture. Circle the **endangered** animals in red and the **ways to protect** them in green.

What Did You Learn?

1. Color the animals that live in this habitat. Circle the animals from your country.

2. Compare the characteristics of these habitats. Follow the example.

light → Habitat A has less light than habitats B and C.

humidity → Habitats ____ and ____ are more humid than habitat ____.

temperature → Habitat ____ is warmer than ____. Habitat ____ is colder than ____.

Final Evaluation

3. Describe one positive and one negative human impact on the environment. Propose a way to correct the negative impact.

a. Positive impact: ____________________

b. Negative impact: ____________________

To correct this we can: ____________________

____

Scientific Skill: Experiment

4. A scientist thought of a question: of an owl, a sheep, a canary and a bat, which animals are **nocturnal**? Remember that **nocturnal** means to sleep during the day and be awake at night. To answer the question, he thought of two procedures:

– Put the animals in a dark room and observe their behavior.
– Go to the forest and observe the animals all day and night.

a. Which procedure is better to answer his question? Explain.

____

____

____

How Did You Do?

For each ☺ color a ⬭.

The Human Body

Key Words

exercise

measure

plan

Day	Activity
Monday	
Tuesday	
Wednesday	
Thursday	
Friday	
Saturday	
Sunday	

protect

pump

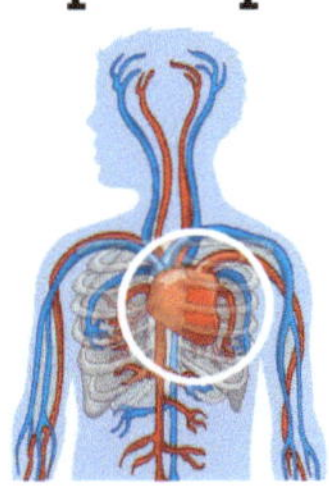

In this unit you will learn to:

- identify the location and function of the heart, lungs and stomach.
- identify the location and function of the skeleton and muscles.
- describe the importance of exercise to develop muscles and strengthen the heart.
- measure using standard and nonstandard units.
- value safety during physical activities.

What Do You Know?

Initial Evaluation

1. Go to **Sticker Set 6** on **page 155**. Put the sticker on the boy's body. Inside our bodies, there are **organs** that work together to keep us alive. Label the organs on the sticker using the letters.

a. heart **b.** lungs **c.** stomach

2. Circle the children who are exercising. Do you think their hearts are **beating fast** or **slowly**?

3. Look at the two girls eating on the bench. Which organ does **food go** to in your body?

____

Scientific Skill: Measure

4. Bones form your **skeleton**. Which bone is the **longest**? Look at the arm and leg bones.

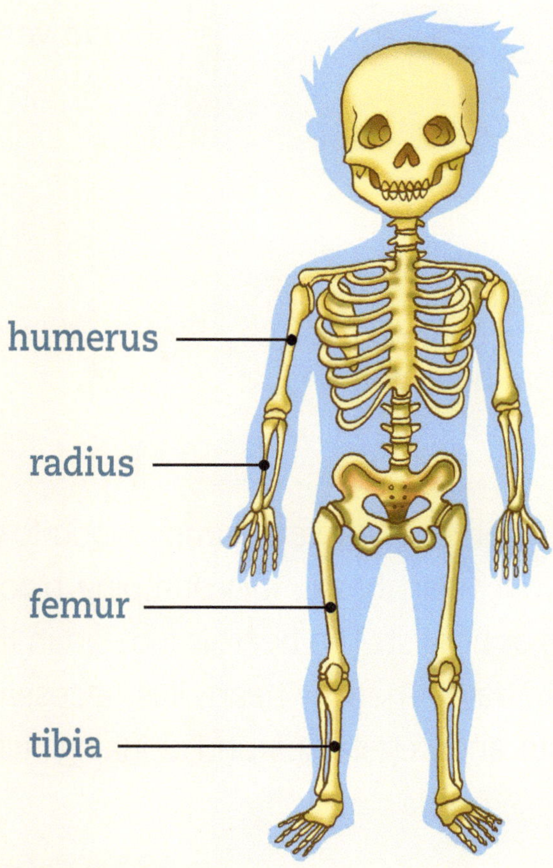

a. Use a pencil to measure your arm and leg bones.

humerus ▶ ☐ pencils.

femur ▶ ☐ pencils.

radius ▶ ☐ pencils.

tibia ▶ ☐ pencils.

b. Which bone is the longest?

____

Section
1 Vital Organs

The Heart

Let's Connect

1. Look at the location of the heart. Answer the questions. Identify

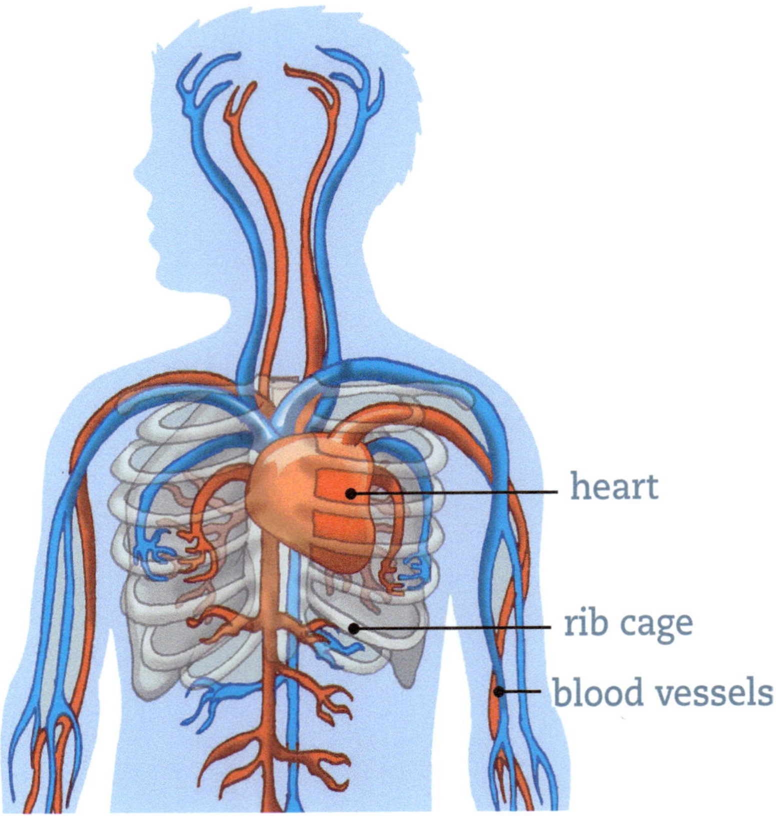

a. Which **structures** are connected to the **heart**?

____

____

b. Which bones **protect** the heart?

____

____

Put your hand on your chest. Can you feel your **heartbeat**?

The **heart** is a very important organ because it keeps us alive. The heart **pumps** blood to all parts of the body through **blood vessels**. Each time your heart beats, it is pumping blood. The heart of each person is about the same size as his or her fist. The heart is located in the **thorax**, and it is protected by the **ribs** of the **rib cage**. To have a healthy heart, it is necessary to eat well by avoiding fat and salt, eating more fruits and vegetables and drinking milk. Exercising is also very good for the heart!

Let's Practice

2. Where is the heart **located**? Mark with a ✔. Identify

☐ In the cranium. ☐ In the thorax. ☐ In the abdomen.

3. What does the **heart** do with **blood**? Explain. Infer

____

____

4. Which child will probably have a healthier heart? Why? Mark with a ✔. Apply

○ 

○ 

Did You Know...?

A baby's heart beats much faster than a child's heart. An adult heartbeat is slower than both, and the heart beats even slower as people get older.

Let's Summarize

The organ that pumps ______________ to all parts of the ______________ is called the ______________. It is located in the thorax and protected by the ______________.

The Lungs

Let's Connect

1. Our heart beats all the time, and we don't even think about it. We also breathe, blink and swallow without telling ourselves to do so. Look at the picture. Answer the questions. Infer

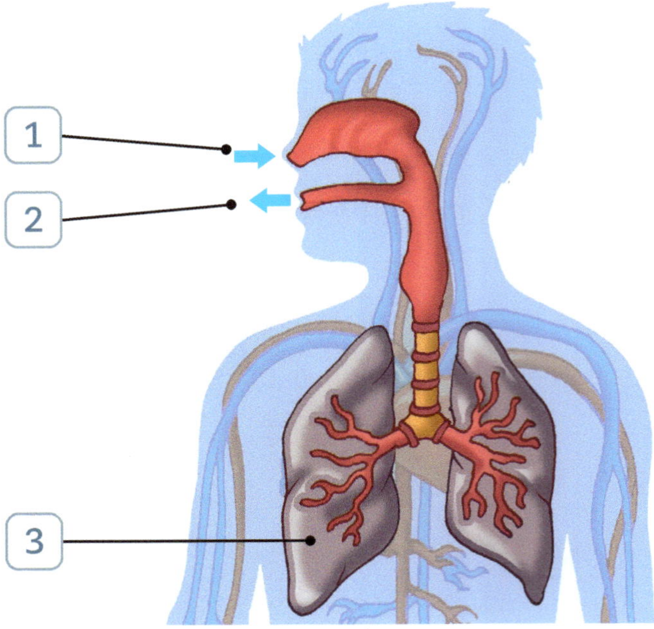

1. **To inhale** is to breathe air through the mouth and nose.
2. **To exhale** is to push air out through the mouth and nose. The air comes out of the body with less oxygen.
3. **Lungs.**

Word Focus

Air is a mix of gases. The most important gas is oxygen. Oxygen is **vital**, meaning it is necessary for life.

a. When we move quickly or jump we need **more oxygen**. Why does exercise make us breathe faster?

____

b. Oxygen is needed in all parts of the body. Which organ helps it get there?

____

The **lungs** are organs that allow us to breathe. They are located in the **thorax** and, like the heart, are also protected by the **rib cage**. When we inhale, **air enters the lungs**, and **oxygen** from the air enters the **blood** through our lungs. The heart pumps the blood to the rest of the body. The lungs absorb the oxygen that the body needs, and then we exhale the same air, but with **less oxygen**.

We need to take care of our lungs. Exercising is good for our lungs because it makes us breathe faster and use more oxygen.

Let's Practice

2. Complete the diagram of the stages of breathing. Describe

inhale

____

____

____

exhale

____

____

____

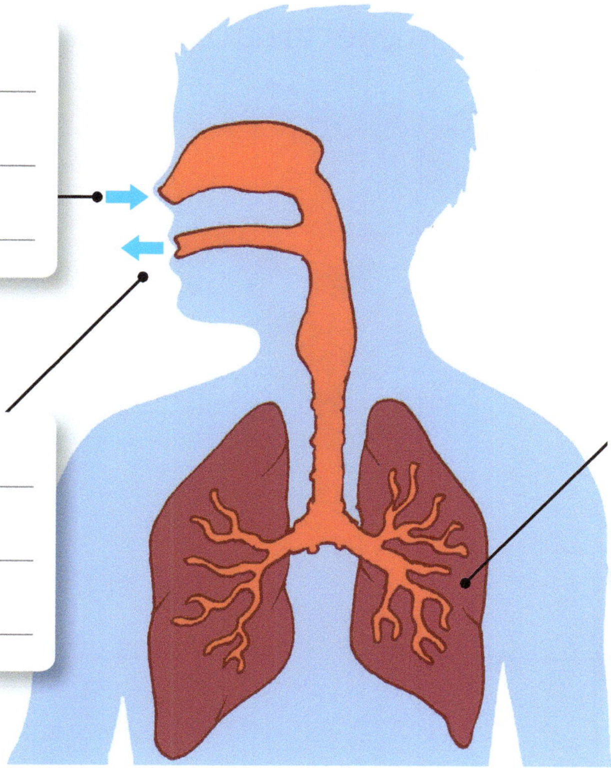

lungs

____

____

____

Challenge

Take a deep breath and blow up a balloon. Hold the end tight so no air escapes. Have your partner do the same. Who can make a bigger balloon?

Tip

Sentence starters:

- When you inhale air...
- When you exhale air...
- The lungs...

3. Where does oxygen go after it enters the lungs? Explain. Infer

____

____

____

Let's Summarize

You use your lungs to...

- exhale air with less ______________________.
- inhale air that contains ______________________. → Then it travels to the ______________________. → Next, it is pumped to the other parts of the body.

The Stomach

Let's Connect

1. Read the children's conversation. Answer the question. Infer

Where does our food go when we eat? I think it goes to the stomach, which is like a bag inside your body.

No, the stomach is a **tube** that goes through our bodies.

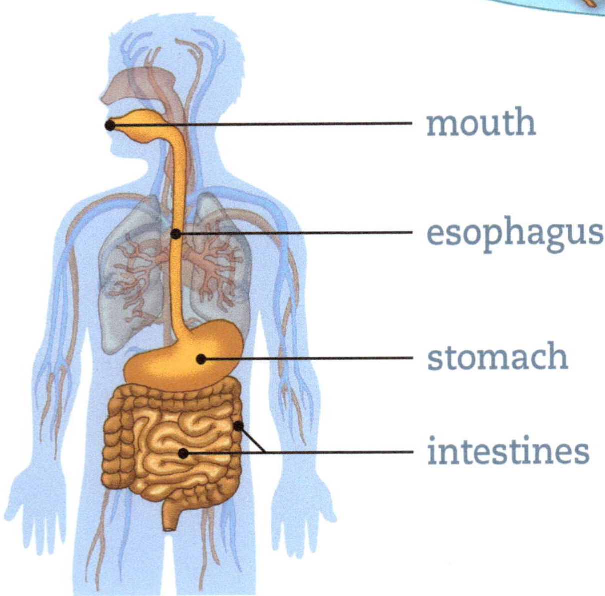

a. Look at the picture of the **digestive system**. Who is correct? Explain your answer.

____

____

____

____

Food gives us the energy for all our daily activities. Food enters through the mouth, where it is chewed into smaller pieces. Then it is swallowed and goes down the esophagus and into the **stomach**.

In the stomach, food is mixed and made into smaller pieces, which then go to the intestines. There, even smaller pieces are absorbed into the blood and then passed to all parts of the body. This process keeps human beings alive.

It is important to eat healthy foods, like fruits and vegetables, and to drink a lot of water. Also, remember to eat slowly and chew your food well.

▶ Identify the location and function of the heart, lungs and stomach

Let's Practice

2. Write **T** for true or **F** for false. Differentiate

a. ☐ The stomach is located next to the heart.

b. ☐ Food is necessary to live.

c. ☐ Food is digested in the stomach.

d. ☐ The stomach is like a bag.

Let's Summarize

Food enters the ______________ and passes through the esophagus to the ______________, where it mixes and transforms. Then it moves to the intestines.

Quiz Yourself

1. Color each of the vital organs a different color. Explain their functions.

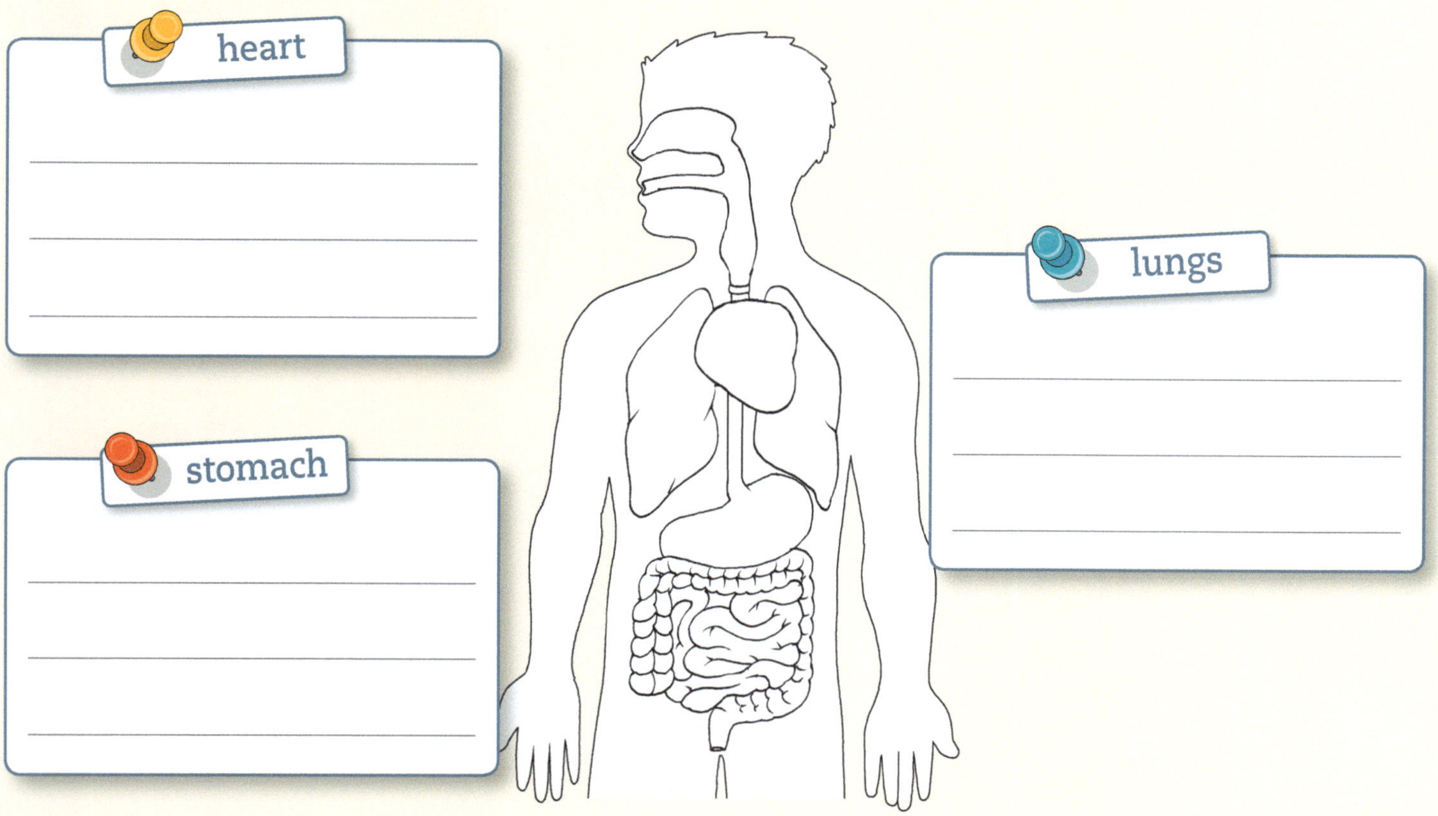

Research Question

When Does My Pulse Change?

What Do I Need?

- a stopwatch

Your pulse is caused by your heartbeat. It is the movement of blood through your body as your heart pumps.

To measure means to find out information by using scientific instruments. You can also use nonscientific units of measurement, like pencils, ice cream sticks and paper clips.

What Do I Do?

Work with a partner. Write the information in the **Results** section.

1. Look at the picture to see how to take your pulse. Put your first two fingers against the side of your neck. Gently press into your neck to find your pulse.
2. Stay seated for 5 minutes. Breathe normally. Then count your pulse for 15 seconds. Your partner will use the stopwatch to time you. Write down the result.
3. Walk for 5 minutes. Then count your pulse for 15 seconds. Write down the result.
4. Run for 5 minutes. Then count your pulse for 15 seconds. Write down the result.
5. Switch with your partner, and record the results.

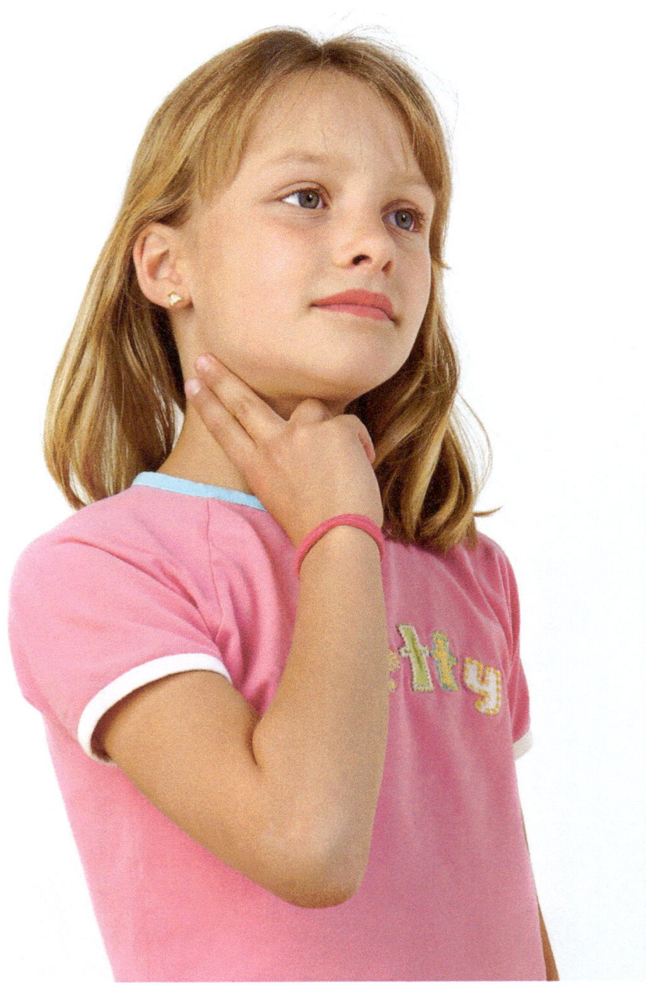

What instrument did you use to measure in this experiment? Is it a scientific instrument?

Results

1. Write your results in the table.

Activity	Pulse Count (15 seconds)	Breathing (fast or slow)
sitting		
after walking		
after running		

2. Make a graph of the data.

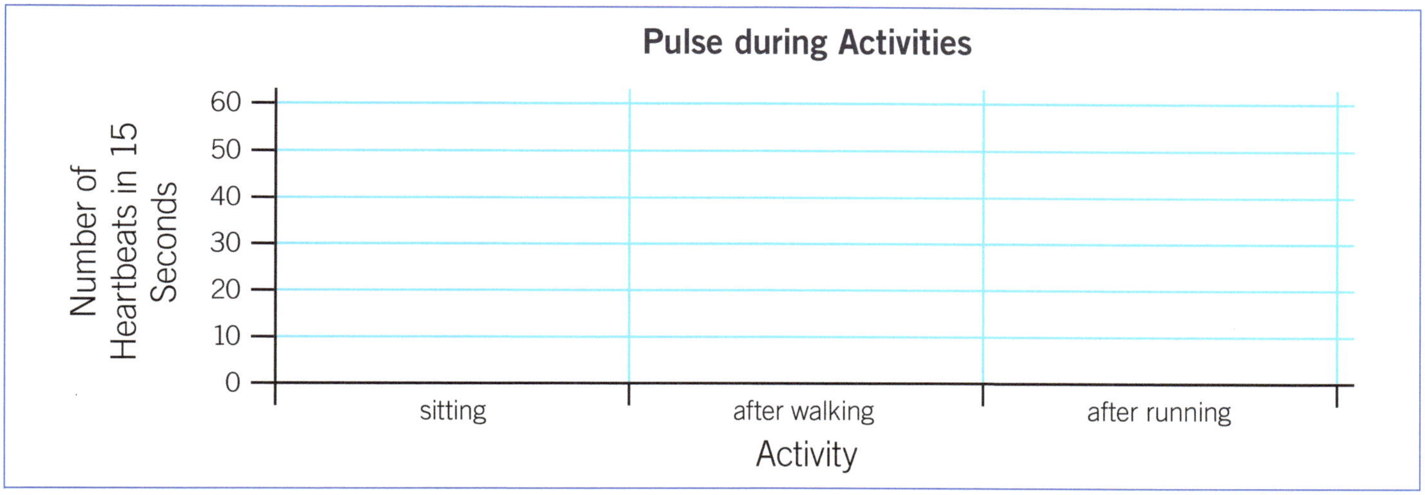

Conclusion

1. How did your pulse change during the activities?

____

2. Why is it important to use a stopwatch in this activity?

____

What you just did was to **measure your pulse using your hand** and **a stopwatch**. In science, all the events we study can be measured in some way.

Section 2

How the Body Moves

The Skeleton

Let's Connect

1. Look at the **bones** that form the human skeleton. Answer the questions. Infer

a. What is the skeleton's **function**?

____

____

b. Which bones do you think protect the **important areas** of the body?

____

____

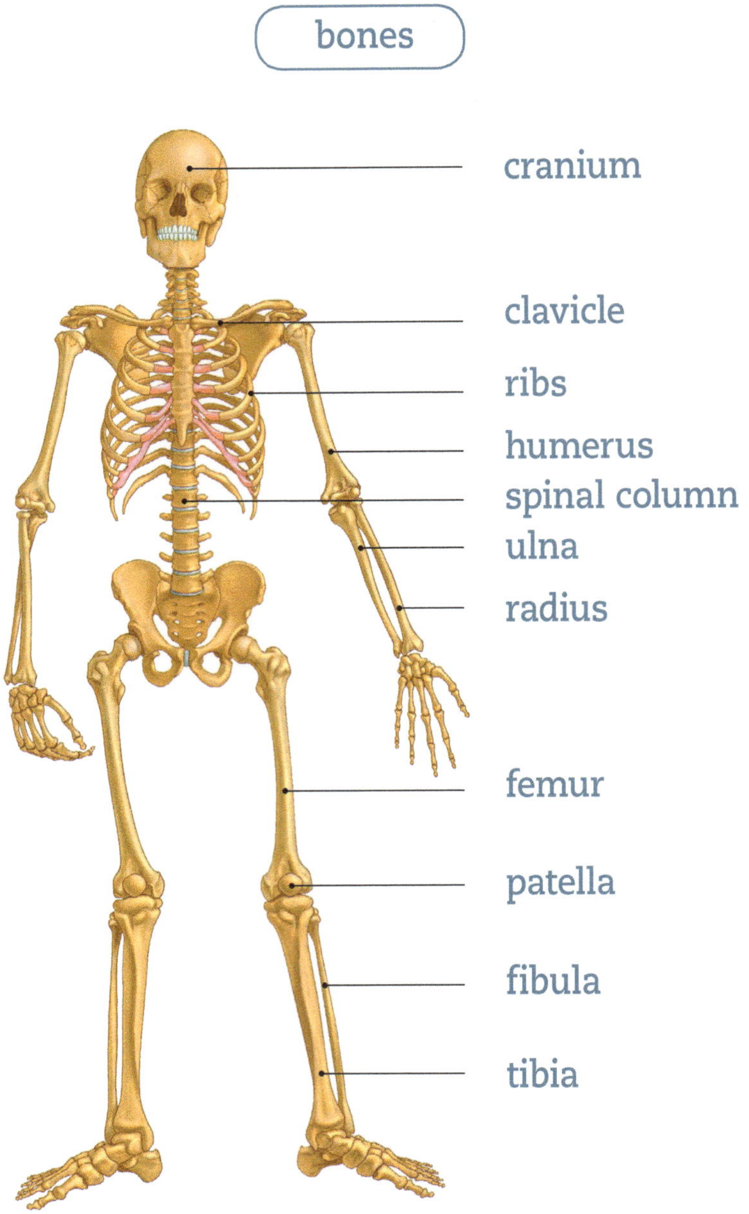

Did You Know...?

You are born with 300–350 bones, but some join together as you grow. Human adults have only 206 bones in their bodies!

The **skeleton supports** and **gives shape** to the body, and together with muscles, it helps us move. Some bones protect important organs. For example, the **cranium** protects the brain, the **rib cage** covers the heart and lungs, and the **spinal column** protects the spinal cord. Bones are connected by **joints**, like knees, elbows, shoulders and hips.

Let's Practice

2. Use the color key to match the body parts with their location. Identify

head   torso   limbs

patella	cranium
humerus	clavicle
radius	rib cage
femur	tibia

Challenge

Sing "Dem Bones" with your friends. Perform it for your class. (Ask your teacher for the music.)

3. Explain the three functions of the skeleton. Identify

____

____

____

____

Did You Know...?

The smallest bones in the body are in the ears. They are called the hammer, the anvil and the stirrup because they look similar to these objects.

Go to **Activity Cards 4** and **5**. Build a human skeleton!

Let's Summarize

The skeleton is made of _______________ (bones / muscles). They _______________ (color / support) and give _______________ (shape / space) to the body, _______________ (protect / connect) vital organs and allow us to _______________ (listen / move).

Muscles

Let's Connect

1. The human body has about 600 muscles, each with a different function. Look at the picture.

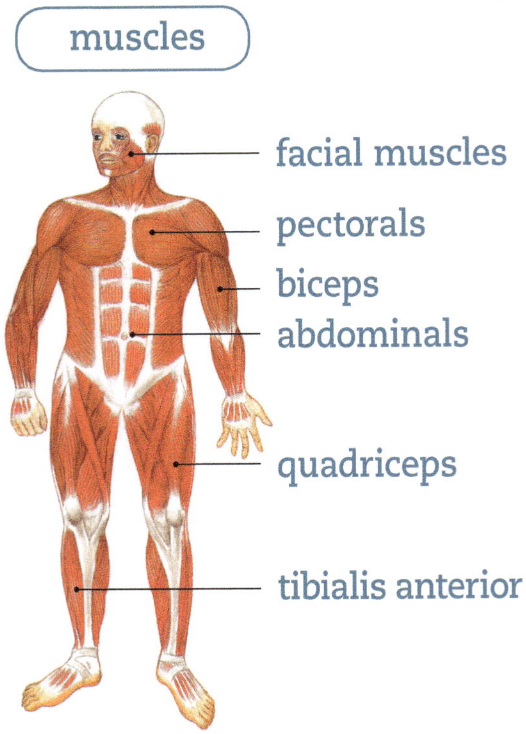

a. Look at the photograph and identify the muscles in your body. Identify

b. Which muscles do you think the gymnast is using? Infer

A **muscle** is an **elastic tissue** that can contract and expand, or shorten and lengthen. Muscles allow us to move in different ways.

Some muscles are **voluntary**, which means we can move them when we want to. For example, our arms and hands allow us to write, and we can make silly expressions with our face. Other muscles are **involuntary**, which means they move on their own without our control. For example, the esophagus muscles push food to our stomach and the heart beats by itself.

To have healthy muscles, you need to exercise regularly and eat well.

Let's Practice

2. Mark the correct muscle functions with a ✔. Identify

☐ Pump blood throughout the body.

☐ Allow movement.

☐ Protect organs.

☐ Digest food.

3. Go to **Cutout 5** on **page 147**. Glue the pictures in the correct boxes. Classify

voluntary muscles

involuntary muscles

Let's Summarize

Bones and ______________________ allow us to move. If we control a muscle's movement, it is called a ______________________ muscle. If we do not control its movement, it is called an ______________________ muscle.

Muscles and Bones Work Together

Let's Connect

1. Our bones support us and, together with our muscles, allow us to move. Look at the picture. Answer the questions. Infer

a. Which **voluntary muscles** are people 2, 3 and 5 using in the picture?

____

____

b. Circle the **joints** used by person 1 and person 4.

Movements allow us to do our daily activities. If our muscles and bones do not function correctly, we will have problems moving or problems with vital bodily functions.

Fun Fact!

Elephants are the only animals that cannot jump. On the other hand, fleas can jump up to 350 times their height!

Education through Values

Some people cannot move their bodies as a result of muscular or bone-related problems. If you see someone in a wheelchair or someone who is having difficulty walking, offer them your help!

Let's Practice

2. Write two involuntary muscular actions. Explain

____

____

____

Let's Summarize

In our bodies the ____________________ and the ____________________ allow us to ____________________.

Quiz Yourself

1. Look at the muscles and bones in the pictures. Complete the activities.

a. Color the muscles and bones you use to jump with (blue).

b. Color the muscles you use to write with (green).

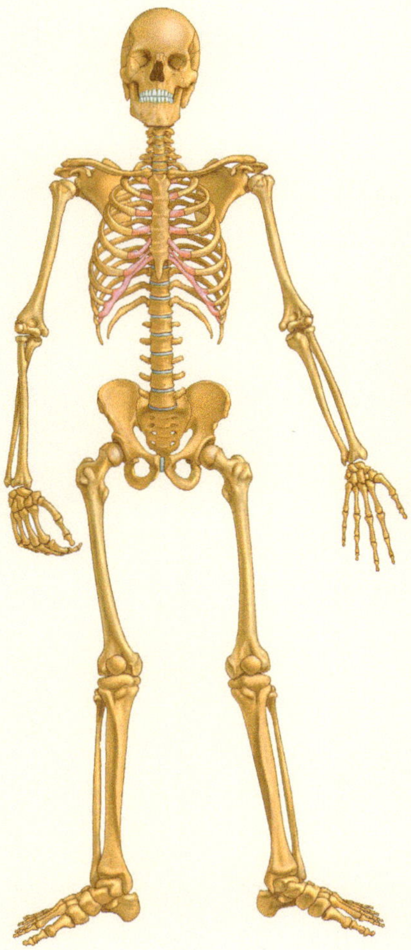

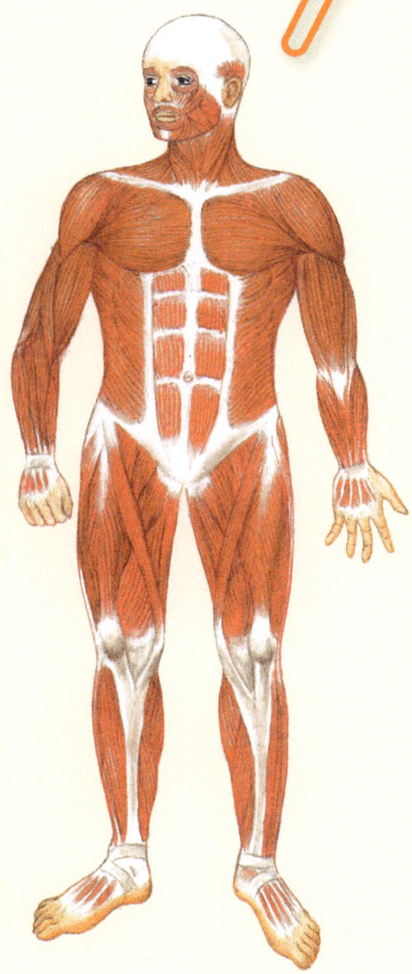

2. What are the functions of bones and muscles?

____

____

____

____

____

Let's Check!

1. Color the organs that each child is using.

situation 1

situation 2

a. Explain the function of the organs you colored.

situation 1 ▶ ______________________________

____

situation 2 ▶ ______________________________

____

2. Which organ sends oxygen to the whole body? Mark the correct answer with a ✓.

A Lungs.

B Heart.

C Stomach.

3. Which organs does the skeleton protect?

____

____

4. Circle the body parts where the muscles and bones are being used the most.

a. Mark the muscles you use to play.

- ◯ voluntary
- ◯ involuntary

b. Mark the organ that the children in the photo are not using.

- ◯ heart
- ◯ lungs
- ◯ stomach

c. How do muscles and bones work together?

____

How Did You Do?

For each ☺ color a ⬭.

Taking Care of Our Bodies

Let's Exercise!

Let's Connect

1. Look at the picture. Follow the instructions. Identify

a. Circle the children who are **taking care of** their bodies in blue.

b. Circle the children who **will harm** their bodies if they continue their actions in red.

Physical activity, like sports and exercise, are part of a **healthy lifestyle**, and they **strengthen** bones and muscles.

After exercising, the **heart beats faster**, which means it is working hard and sending blood quickly to all parts of the body. Every time you run, ride a bike or do other exercise, you are helping your body stay healthy. You are also **developing muscles** that will help you grow and be strong.

Let's Practice

2. Imagine that these children repeat these actions often. Mark the actions that have positive effects with a ✔. Mark the negative actions for the heart and muscles with an ✘. Identify

3. Why is it important to exercise and eat healthy food? Explain

____

____

____

Let's Summarize

To stay healthy, you should ____________________ because it strengthens your ____________________ and ____________________.

Exercise Plan

Let's Connect

1. Look at the pictures. Follow the instructions. Identify

a. Mark the activity you like to do the **most**.

b. How **often** do you do it?

____

We already know that exercise is important for the body.
To make a **habit** of exercising, consider the following:

- you should spend a maximum of two hours a day sitting down.
- watching TV or using the computer are activities that you usually do sitting down.
- if you have a bicycle, use it every day—even for just half an hour.
- play outside whenever you can. You can jump rope, play soccer or run races.

Staying Healthy

Smoking is very harmful to the smoker and everyone around. Ask smokers you know to try and quit smoking and, if they are going to smoke, not to smoke around nonsmokers.

Let's Practice

2. Make an exercise calendar for next week. Write down what you want to do each day to develop your muscles and strengthen your heart. Show it to your physical education teacher so he or she can help you meet your goals. Design

Day	Activity
Monday	
Tuesday	
Wednesday	
Thursday	
Friday	
Saturday	
Sunday	

Let's Summarize

It is important to make an exercise ______________________ to keep your ______________________ healthy.

Quiz Yourself

1. How does exercise help:

a. Your muscles? ______________________

______________________.

b. Your heart? ______________________

______________________.

What Did You Learn?

1. Color the organs. Use the key.

heart

lungs

stomach

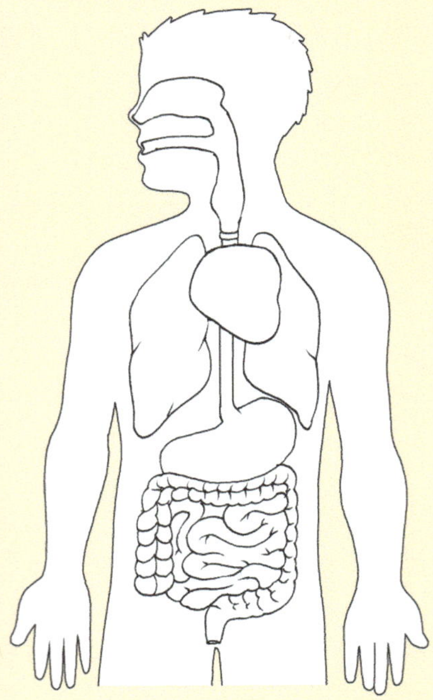

a. Explain the function of each organ.

The heart: ______________________________

____

The lungs: ______________________________

____

The stomach: ______________________________

____

2. How do the muscles and skeleton function? Mark the correct answer with a ✓.

A The muscles support the body, and the skeleton protects it.

B The muscles protect the organs, and the skeleton pumps blood.

C The muscles and the skeleton work together to move the body.

3. Why is exercise important for the muscles and the heart?

____

____

4. For this activity you will need string, scissors and an ice cream stick.

- Exhale and use string to measure your rib cage. Cut the string in the correct spot (measurement 1).
- Breathe deeply and hold the air in your lungs. Measure your rib cage again (measurement 2).
- Place both pieces of string on the desk. Measure them using the ice cream stick.

measurement 1	measurement 2
______ ice cream sticks.	______ ice cream sticks.

a. Are the measurements the same? Explain what happened.

____

____

How Did You Do?

For each ☺ color a ⬭.

Unit 4

Water

Key Words

container

temperature

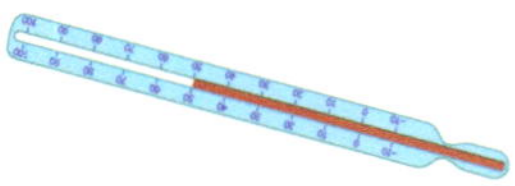

faucet

liquid

pollution

In this unit you will learn to:

- describe the properties of water.
- compare the physical states of water.
- describe the water cycle and value water as a natural resource.
- use scientific materials and instruments correctly.
- value water as an important part of life.

What Do You Know?

Initial Evaluation

1. Look at the picture. Circle.

two **solids** two **liquids** two **gases**

2. What happens when you put sugar in coffee? Mark the correct answer.

- [ ] It makes the coffee hot.
- [ ] It makes the coffee solid.
- [ ] It makes the coffee cold.
- [ ] It dissolves in the coffee.

Scientific Skill: Use instruments

3. Jason wants to know how much water is in a glass. Go to **Sticker Set 7** on **page 155**. Stick the picture of the correct instrument in the box.

a. Stick the other instruments here. Describe how they are used.

Properties of Water

Observing Water

Let's Connect

1. Work with a partner. For this activity, you will need water, a glass, paper with something written on it, three different containers, a tray, a dropper and oil. Infer

a. Fill the glass with water. Hold the paper behind the glass and try to read it. What **color** is the water? Can you read what is written on the paper? How does the text look?

b. Pour water in the three different containers. What **shape** does the water have? Does its shape change or **adapt** to the container? If you put the water in a new container, would the water adapt its shape again?

c. Put a drop of water and a drop of oil separately on the tray. **Tilt** the tray. Closely observe what happens. Which drop **moves** first?

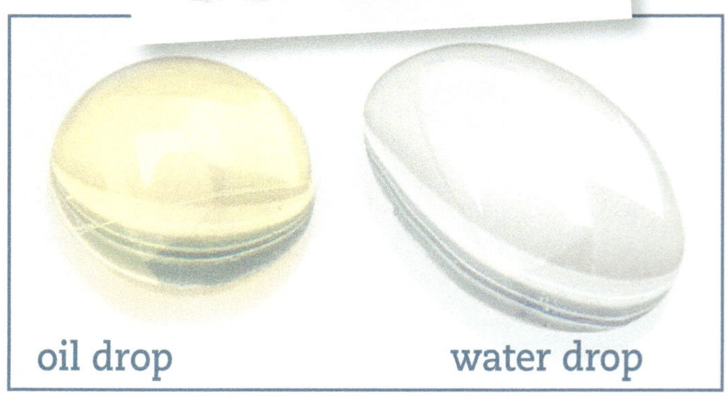

Be careful when handling glass because it can easily break and cut you.

Water is a very important liquid. All living things need water to survive, and some plants and animals live in water.
The properties of water include being **tasteless**, **odorless**, **colorless** and **transparent**. Transparent means you can see through it. It also has the ability to **flow**, to **adapt** to the shape of the space it occupies and to **drain** or move quickly.

Word Focus

Less: when less is added to the end of a word it means "without." For example, careless means "without care."

Let's Practice

2. Mark the properties of water with a ✔. Identify

☐ It is odorless.	☐ It is tasteless.	☐ It is transparent.
☐ It has color.	☐ It flows.	☐ It does not flow.
☐ It has a taste.	☐ It is colorless.	☐ It has a smell.
☐ It adapts.	☐ It drains.	☐ It does not adapt.

Let's Summarize

Water

It has no taste or smell. This means it is ______________ and ______________.	You can see through it. This means it is ______________.	It has no color. This means it is ______________.	It ______________ to the container it is in, and it can ______________ and ______________.

Learning about Water

Let's Connect

1. Work with a partner. You need four plastic cups, water, sugar, salt, juice powder, rice, and a spoon. Infer

Fill the cups with water. Add sugar to the first cup, juice powder to the second, salt to the third and rice to the fourth. Mix them with the spoon.

a. What happens? How are the results different? Why do you think the results are different?

2. Look at the pictures. Discuss with a classmate. Infer

a. What happens to the water in the pictures?

b. Are the changes related to temperature? Explain.

Another property of water is that it is a **solvent**. This means it **dissolves**, or **breaks down**, solids to create a mixture, or solution.

Water's **physical state changes** when it is exposed to different temperatures. When water is exposed to high temperatures, it **evaporates**, transforming into **water vapor**, a **gas**. When exposed to very low temperatures, it **freezes**, becoming a **solid** in the form of ice.

Let's Practice

3. Write **T** for true and **F** for false. Compare and contrast

a. ☐ Water can dissolve sugar.

b. ☐ Water evaporates when exposed to high temperatures.

c. ☐ Water from the faucet comes out as a gas.

d. ☐ Water freezes when exposed to very low temperatures.

Let's Summarize

Water ______________________ some solids, like sugar and salt. Also, if we expose water to changes in ______________, it ______________ or ______________.

Quiz Yourself

1. Look at the children working in the lab. List the **properties** they are testing.

____

____

____

____

____

____

____

____

Section

2 Physical States of Water

Solid, Liquid and Gas

Let's Connect

1. Look at the image. Do the activities. Identify

a. Circle water in a **solid state** in (blue).

b. Circle water in a **liquid state** in (green).

c. Circle water in a **gaseous state** in (yellow).

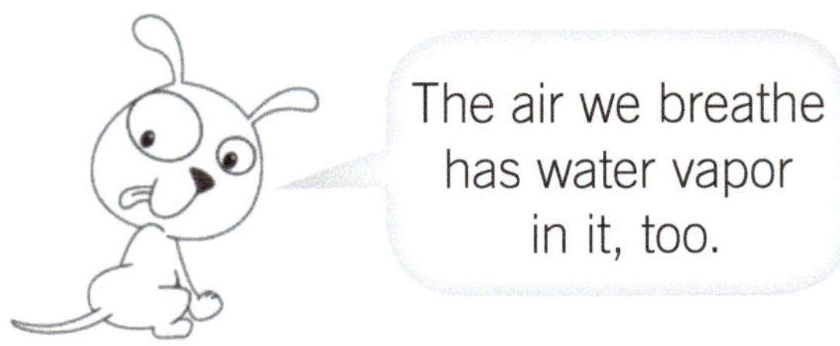

In nature, water can be found in three states: **solid (ice)**, **liquid** and **gas (vapor)**. Each state has different properties.

Let's Practice

2. Write an **S** next to water as a **solid**, an **L** next to water as a **liquid** and a **G** next to water as a **gas**. Identify

Did You Know...?

If the earth were divided in four parts, almost three of them would be water. Most of the water on earth is salty and forms the oceans and seas.

Let's Summarize

In nature, water can be found in three states:

______________________, ______________________ and ______________________.

How Water Transforms

Let's Connect

1. Look at the picture. Answer the questions.

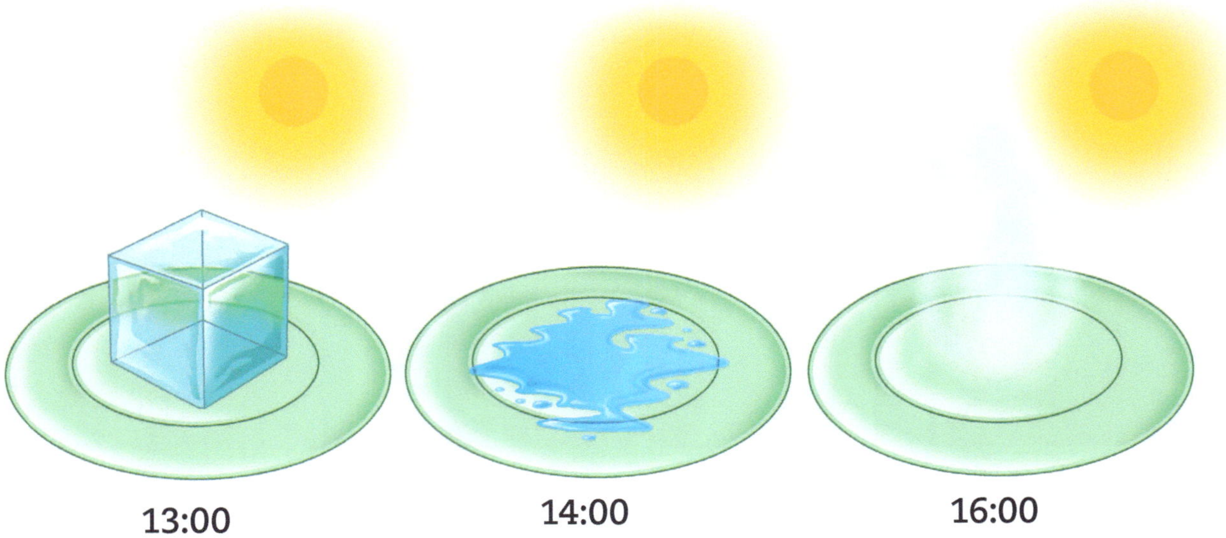

a. What is the **physical state** of the water on each plate? Identify

13:00 ▶ ____________ 14:00 ▶ ____________ 16:00 ▶ ____________

b. Why did the **ice** change? Infer

____

The physical state of water changes with the temperature (T°).

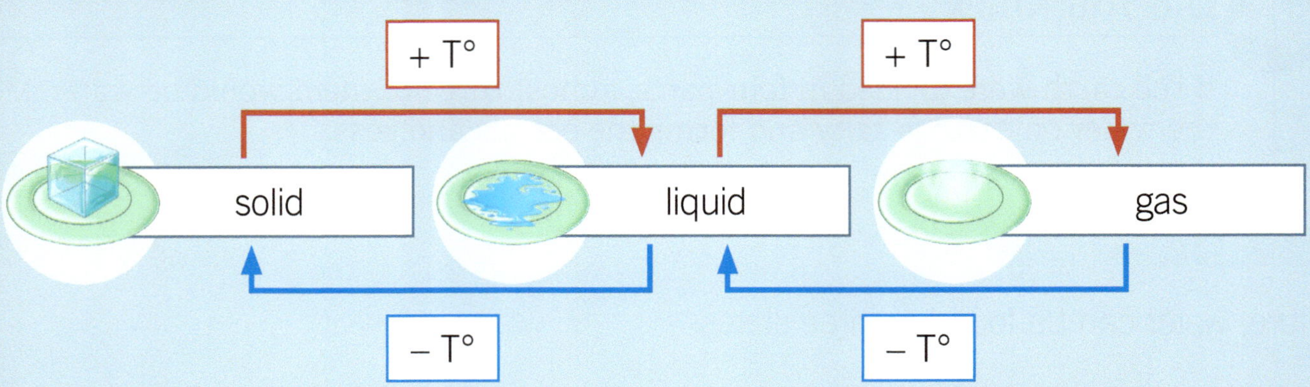

Let's Practice

2. Use different colors to match the **situations** with the **states** of water. Infer

Liquid exposed to **increasing** temperatures.	ice	Liquid exposed to **decreasing** temperatures.
Vapor exposed to **decreasing** temperatures.	liquid	Ice exposed to **increasing** temperatures.
	gas	

Let's Summarize

Water can be in different states: solid, liquid or gas. Water changes state when exposed to different temperatures. Go to **Cutout 6** on **page 147**. Glue the pictures in the correct boxes.

Water at a high temperature.	Water at a moderate temperature.	Water at a low temperature.

Did You Know...?

Global warming is the rise of environmental temperatures. It transforms glaciers and ice into liquid, causing thousands of animals in the North and South Poles to lose their habitats. Pollution from automobiles and industry is one of the main causes of global warming.

Comparing States of Water

Let's Connect

1. For this activity, you need two plastic bottles and water. Infer

Fill the bottles up halfway with water and put the bottle caps on. Put one bottle in the freezer, and leave the other at room temperature. Wait two hours. Observe and compare.

a. What are the **characteristics** of water in its liquid and solid forms? How are they **different**?

____

____

b. If you put ice in a bottle and leave it **in the sun**, how will the ice **change**?

____

____

Every physical state of water has **distinct characteristics**. Ice has a defined shape, liquid adapts its shape, and vapor rises and expands in the available space.

Go to **Activity Cards 6** and **7**. Play dominoes with a partner.

Let's Practice

2. Look at the pictures. Do the activities. Identify

________________ ________________ ________________

a. Write the form of the water on each cup.

b. Write the name of the **physical state** under each picture.

c. Which picture shows water that is **adapting** to the shape of the cup? Mark it with a ✔.

☐ 1 ☐ 2 ☐ 3

Let's Summarize

The **physical states** of water are different. Ice has a ________________ shape, liquid ________________ its shape to the container it is in, and vapor expands, rises and occupies the available ________________.

Quiz Yourself

1. Complete the table with **yes** or **no**.

	Ice	Liquid	Vapor
Has a defined shape			
Occupies available space			
Adapts its shape			

Research Question

What Temperature is the Water?

What Do I Need?

- 3 measuring cups
- water
- ice
- warm water
- an alcohol thermometer
- a stopwatch

It is important to use an alcohol thermometer. Other thermometers have mercury and can be very dangerous if they break.

Learning how to **use instruments** means using them correctly and knowing the **functions** and **risks** of each instrument. Caution! Before using instruments, be sure to take safety **precautions**, especially when working with dangerous materials like glass.

What Do I Do?

1. Fill the first measuring cup with cold water, the second with ice and the third with warm water. Your teacher will help you.
2. Measure the temperature by putting the thermometer in each cup for one minute. Record the temperatures.

Results

1. Color the thermometers using the information you recorded.

Cold water:

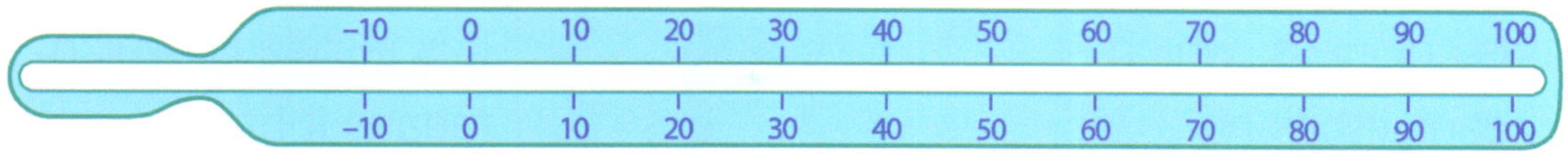

Ice:

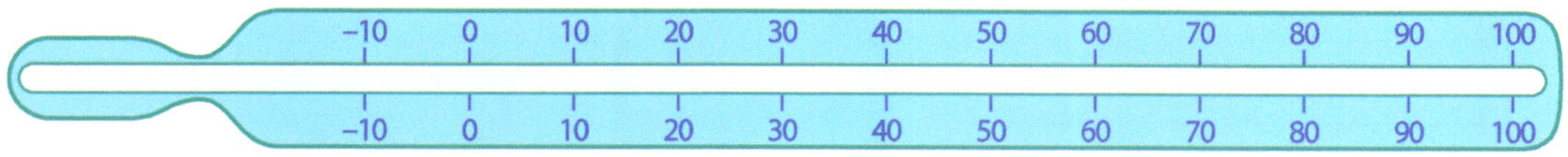

Warm water:

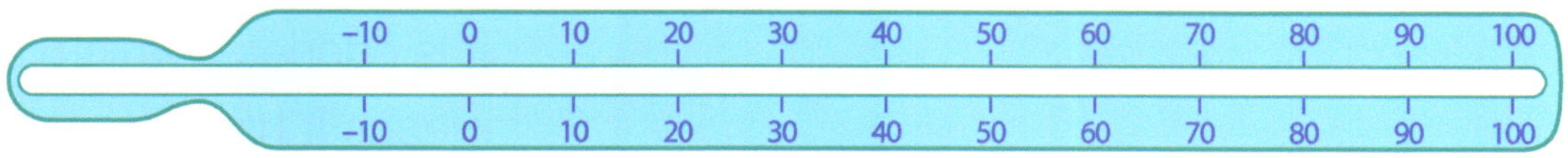

2. Was the temperature in each cup different? Why?

____

____

Conclusion

1. Which of the concepts in this unit are related to this experiment?

____

____

2. What was the purpose of the instruments you used? What precautions did you take?

____

____

The experiment used **scientific instruments** and **materials**. To use these instruments correctly, you should always know their functions and risks, and the precautions you should take when using them.

Let's Check!

1. Complete the properties of water.

It is colorless, which means it has no ________________.

It can adapt its ________________, ________________ and ________________.

It can ________________ some solids, like sugar and salt.

It is tasteless, which means it has no ________________.

It is odorless, which means it has no ________________.

It is transparent, which means you can ________________ it.

Mark the correct answers with a ✔.

2. What is the physical state of water as ice?

- A Solid.
- B Liquid.
- C Gas.

3. What causes liquid to become vapor?

- A Decreasing temperatures.
- B Increasing temperatures.
- C Moderate temperatures.

4. Write one similarity and one difference for each pair of photographs.

similarity ▶ ______________________

difference ▶ ______________________

similarity ▶ ______________________

difference ▶ ______________________

similarity ▶ ______________________

difference ▶ ______________________

How Did You Do?

For each ☺ color a ⬭.

Section 3
Keeping Water Clean

The Water Cycle

Let's Connect

1. Have you ever thought about how water forms clouds? Or why it rains? Write the correct numbers in the circles to put the water cycle in order. Sequence

(1) **Evaporation**: The sun heats bodies of water like oceans, rivers and lakes, transforming the water into vapor.

(2) **Condensation**: As the vapor rises, the air gets colder. The vapor then transforms into small drops of water, which form clouds.

(3) **Solidification**: Some of the drops of water in clouds freeze and become snow or hail.

(4) **Precipitation**: Water falls from the clouds as rain (liquid), or as snow or hail (solids).

(5) **Snowmelt/Runoff**: Ice melts and becomes water. It joins rainwater running off land and forms rivers, which return the water to lakes and oceans.

(6) **Infiltration**: Some water soaks into the ground and forms underground bodies of water.

(7) Plants and animals consume water to live. They eliminate water through respiration, transpiration, urine and feces.

Since water exists in different states, it can be found underground and in the air, glaciers, oceans, rivers and lakes. All this water is part of the **water cycle** or **hydrologic cycle**. The water cycle is a **closed cycle**, which means the total amount of water is always the same.

Let's Practice

2. Match the descriptions with the correct stages of the water cycle. Identify

Water becomes vapor and rises. ○	○ **condensation** (gas to liquid)
Snow and hail form. ○	○ **evaporation** (liquid to gas)
Clouds form. ○	○ **solidification** (liquid to solid)
Snow and hail melt. ○	○ **snowmelt** (solid to liquid)

Let's Summarize

Describe the stage of the water cycle that relates to each picture.

Water Pollution

Let's Connect

1. Look at the diagram. Answer the questions with a classmate. Infer

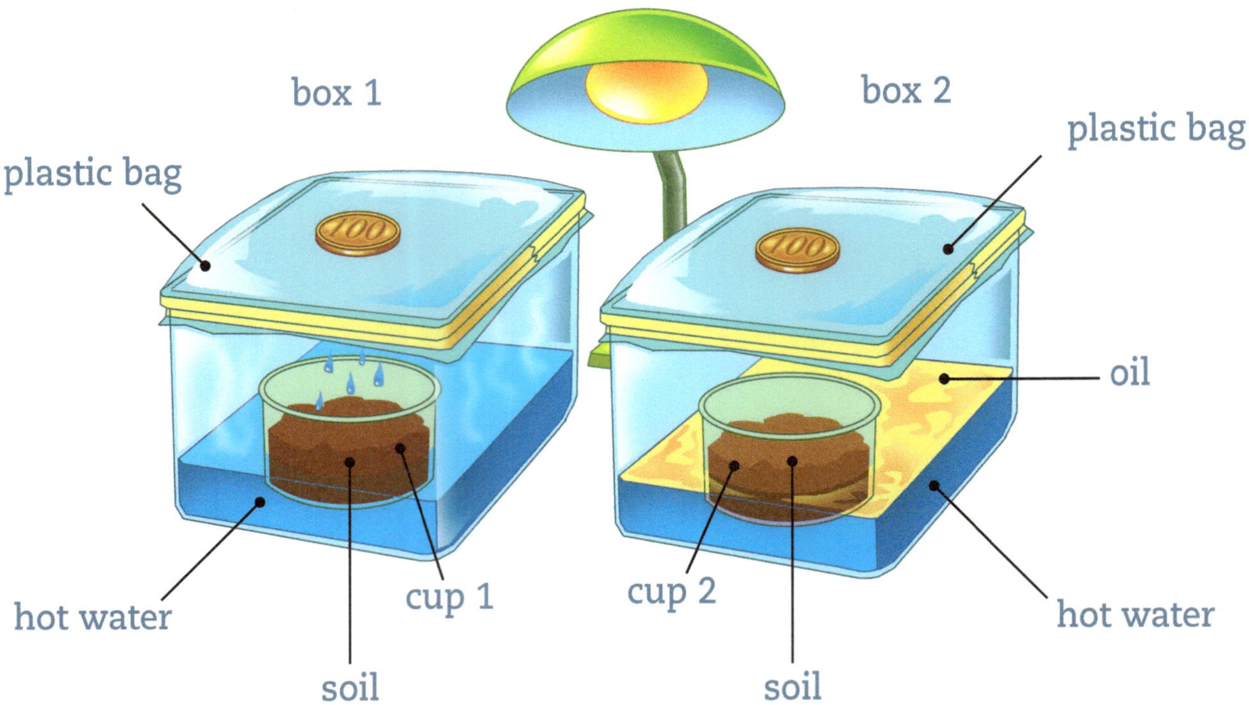

a. Why do **water drops fall** in cup 1? Does the same happen in cup 2?

b. Which part of the water cycle does the diagram represent?

c. Petroleum is represented by the oil. Why do you think petroleum **spills** damage the ocean?

Every day we drink and use water. Unfortunately, a lot of the water on earth is already **polluted** because of human activities. These can be **domestic activities**, like washing cars with soap; **agricultural activities**, like using pesticides; and **industrial activities**, like dumping waste in the ocean.

Let's Practice

2. Look at the picture. Color the activities that pollute water in [orange]. Identify

Education through Values

Oil is a water **pollutant**. A little bit of oil can pollute a large amount of water. After cooking with oil, **do not pour it down the drain**. You should fill up a container with oil and throw it away or add it to a compost bin. This way you are helping protect the earth's water supply.

Word Focus

A **pollutant** is a foreign substance that contaminates or makes something less pure.

Let's Summarize

Which human activities are the **primary** causes of water pollution?

A Livestock farming, agriculture and fishing.

B Domestic activity, agriculture and industry.

C Fishing, agriculture and mining.

Challenge

Write a three-minute skit that teaches people about one cause of water pollution.

Don't Waste Water!

Let's Connect

1. Match the pictures with the water **conservation** solutions. Identify

Did You Know...?

Fresh water has no salt and is found in lakes and rivers. It is easier to make fresh water safe for humans to drink than salt water from the ocean.

Use a cup to rinse your toothbrush instead of letting the water run.

Fill the sink with water and soap to wash dishes instead of letting the water run.

Fix leaky faucets.

Place a container in the shower while the water heats up. Then use it to water plants.

Earth is also called the "blue planet" because it is mostly water. However, there is very little **fresh water** to drink. That is why it is necessary to **conserve water** and **keep it clean**. Ninety-seven percent of all water is salt water, and three percent is fresh water.

Let's Practice

2. Mark with a ✔ the picture that shows someone conserving water. Identify

Let's Summarize

There is very little fresh water on earth. That is why we should ______________ water by ______________, ______________ and ______________.

Quiz Yourself

1. Look at the picture. Circle stages of the water cycle in [blue]. Write in your notebook the actions that **protect** or **conserve** water and those that **waste** or **contaminate** it.

What Did You Learn?

1. Complete the sentences.

a. Water is ______________________________, meaning it has no color.

b. Liquid water ______________________________ to the shape of the container it is in.

c. Water __________________________ when exposed to high temperatures.

d. Water is ______________________________, meaning it has no smell.

e. Water is ______________________________, meaning you can see through it.

2. What is the difference between the two states of water in the photographs? Explain.

mountains

river

____

____

____

Final Evaluation

3. Write and describe the stages of the water cycle.

____

____

____

____

4. What can you do to conserve or protect water? Mark the correct answer with a ✔.

A Pour oil down the drain.

B Leave the water running.

C Shower in less time.

Scientific Skill: Use instruments

5. What should you know about a scientific instrument in order to use it correctly? Give two examples.

____

____

How Did You Do?

For each ☺ color a ⬭.

Unit 5

Weather

Key Words

season

environment

storm

communicate

In this unit you will learn to:

- describe weather characteristics and how they change during the year.
- measure weather characteristics with scientific instruments.
- recognize the effects of weather changes on living things.
- understand the effects weather and seasons have on living things.
- communicate and record scientific observations and measurements.
- recognize the importance of protecting your skin from the sun.

What Do You Know?

Initial Evaluation

1. Look at the picture and answer.

a. What **season** is it? What are the characteristics of this season?

____

____

b. Circle the children that are **not dressed correctly** for the weather.

c. Go to **Sticker Set 8** on **page 157**. Dress the children correctly.

Scientific Skill: Communicate

2. In science, it is important to **communicate** what you observe and investigate.

The table shows the weather **forecast** for your city. Tomorrow a friend will visit you. Write to your friend about the weather, and suggest what clothes to wear.

	Weather Forecast				
	Monday (today)	Tuesday	Wednesday	Thursday	Friday
Low Temperature (°C)	12	11	8	6	4
High Temperature (°C)	30	27	24	18	22

____

____

____

Section 1

Weather Characteristics

Temperature

Let's Connect

1. Look at the picture. Answer the questions. Interpret

a. Where does the family live? What will the temperature be tomorrow?

____

Word Focus

The **atmosphere** is the layer of gases surrounding the earth.

The **weather** or **climate** is the state of the **atmosphere** in a certain place on earth. Some characteristics of weather are **temperature**, **wind** and **precipitation**. When the temperature is **low,** the weather is **cold**, and when the temperature is **high,** the weather is **warm** or **hot**. The weather can be:

 sunny  partly sunny  cloudy  rainy

Let's Practice

2. Look at the pictures. Mark the **environment** you like more. Describe

▲ Yellowstone National Park

▲ Mojave Desert

a. Describe the **temperature** and **correct clothing** for each environment.

environment 1

____

____

____

environment 2

____

____

____

In general, the temperature is higher during the day than at night and **lower** in the **winter** than in the **summer**.

Challenge

Make a poster of the perfect environment for you. Include the temperature, weather and yourself wearing correct clothing. Use pictures, magazines, fabric and yarn.

Let's Summarize

One characteristic of ______________________ is the ______________________ of each environment, which is related to hot and cold.

Wind and Precipitation

Let's Connect

1. Go to **Cutout 7** on **page 149**. Create the scene in the box. Answer the questions. Identify

a. What happens to the child's hat in the picture? Mark the correct answers.

- [ ] It **flies away** because of the rain.
- [ ] It **flies away** because of the wind.
- [ ] It **gets wet** because of the rain.
- [ ] It **gets wet** because of the wind.

b. Besides the **wind**, what other characteristics can you see? What are the **consequences**? Discuss with a classmate.

Remember!

We learned about precipitation in unit 4.

Wind is a stream of air that comes from the atmosphere. In the picture, wind is **blowing** the leaves off the tree. Another weather characteristic is **precipitation**, which is water or ice that comes from clouds. Precipitation can be **rain**, **hail** or **snow**.

Let's Practice

2. Draw **branches** on the tree. What does the wind do to the branches? Describe

3. Write the name of each type of precipitation. Write if it is **water** or **ice**. Identify

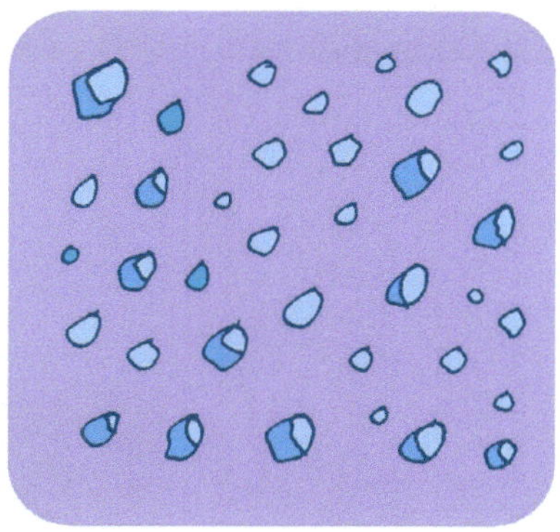

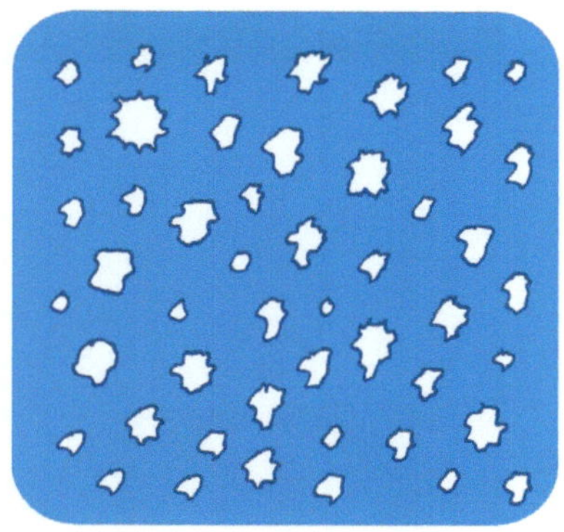

Did You Know...?

The Atacama Desert in Chile is the driest place in the world. It receives only one millimeter of rain a year!

Let's Summarize

Weather Characteristics

- temperature
-
-

The Four Seasons

Let's Connect

1. The pictures are of the same place at different times of the year. Observe how the weather changes. Do the activities. Infer

a. Write the names of the seasons: spring, summer, fall, winter.

b. What are the differences between fall and spring?

Word Focus

The season **fall** is also called **autumn**. Why do you think it is called **fall**?

The weather **changes throughout the year**. Typically, the temperature is hot in summer and cold in winter. In the northern hemisphere, winter is from November to January, and summer is from June to August. In the southern hemisphere, the seasons are the other way around.

Let's Practice

2. Complete the table with the weather characteristics where you live. Compare

Weather Characteristics	Does it change during the year? (yes or no)	Increases or Decreases
Temperature		
Wind		
Precipitation		

Let's Summarize

Weather characteristics ______________________ during the year.

Go to **Activity Card 8**. Find a weather forecast for your area.

Quiz Yourself

1. Describe the **weather** in your area **right now**. Think about the temperature, wind and precipitation.

____

____

____

a. Describe how the weather will change **six months** from now.

____

____

____

Weather Instruments

The Thermometer, Anemometer and Weather Vane

Let's Connect

1. Look at the weather instruments. Answer the question. Infer

weather vane
This instrument shows the **wind direction**.

thermometer
This instrument measures the **temperature** in **Celsius** (or **Fahrenheit)**. The hotter it is, the higher the number on the thermometer.

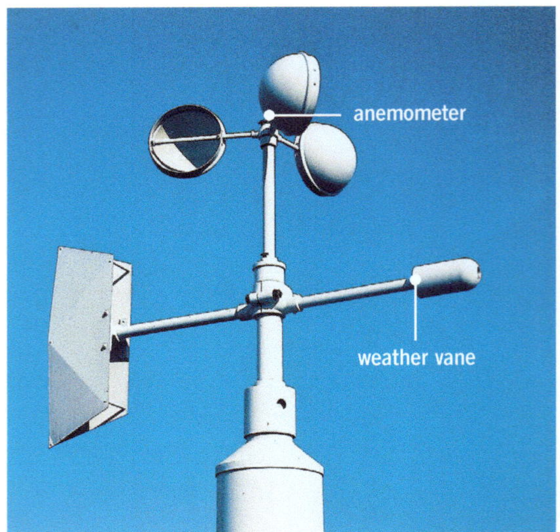

Another weather instrument is the **anemometer**. It measures **wind speed**.

a. Why is the woman surprised by the weather?

____

____

There are many instruments that measure weather, such as the **thermometer**, the **anemometer** and the **weather vane**.

Fun Fact!

Fahrenheit is used only in the United States, the Cayman Islands and Belize.

Let's Practice

2. Construct an anemometer with a classmate. Construct

- Supplies: four plastic cups, two pieces of cardboard, a pencil, tape, scissors, a marker, a clock and a pin.
- Cross the two pieces of cardboard and stick the pin through the middle. Be careful, and ask an adult for help.
- Make two cuts on opposite sides of each cup.
- Tape a cup onto the end of each piece of cardboard, as shown in the picture.
- Mark one cup with a pen to count the rotations of your anemometer.

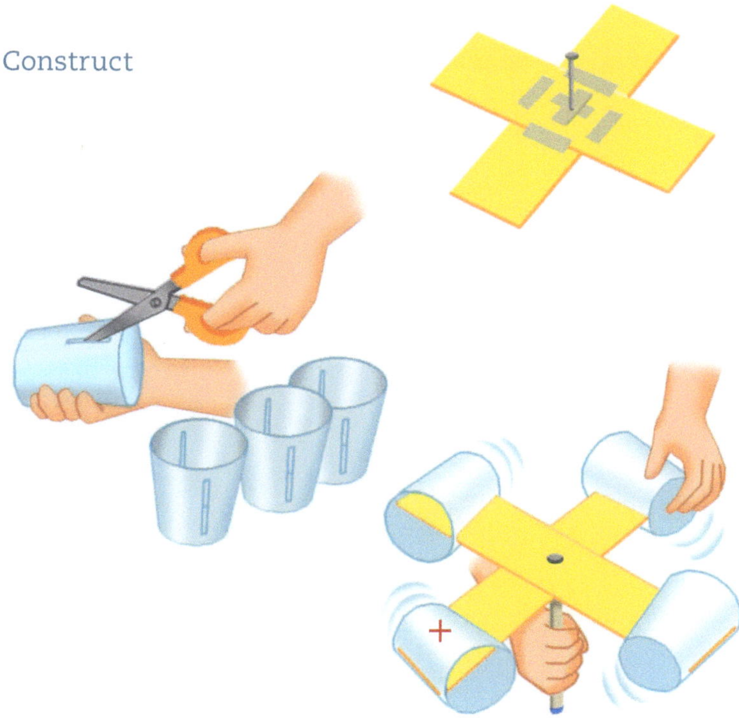

3. Place your **anemometer** in the school yard. How many times does it **rotate** in three minutes? Measure

It rotated ☐ times in three minutes.

4. Is there wind? Is it **strong** or **mild**? Discuss with your class. Compare

5. With your teacher, measure the temperature outside with a **thermometer**. Measure

It is ☐ °C.

Tip

Read the symbol "°" as "degrees."

Let's Summarize

Weather is measured using different instruments. The ____________ measures temperature, the ____________ measures wind speed, and the ____________ measures wind direction.

Pluviometer

Let's Connect

1. You will make a scientific instrument to measure **precipitation**. Construct

Supplies:

- a large glass jar
- a funnel
- a 20 cm ruler
- tape

Tape the ruler to the jar. Make sure the "0" is at the bottom.

Tape the funnel on top of the jar.

a. On a rainy day, place your instrument in the school yard or outside your house. If it does not rain very often where you live, use a water hose to simulate **heavy** or **light** rain. Measure

A **pluviometer** is used to measure **precipitation**. It shows the amount of water—in the form of rain, hail or snow—that falls in a certain place.

Let's Practice

2. The table shows precipitation in different parts of the world. Use the information to complete the graph. Represent

Place	Precipitation (mm)
Lima	0
Barcelona	50
New Orleans	150
Tokyo	200
Mumbai	550

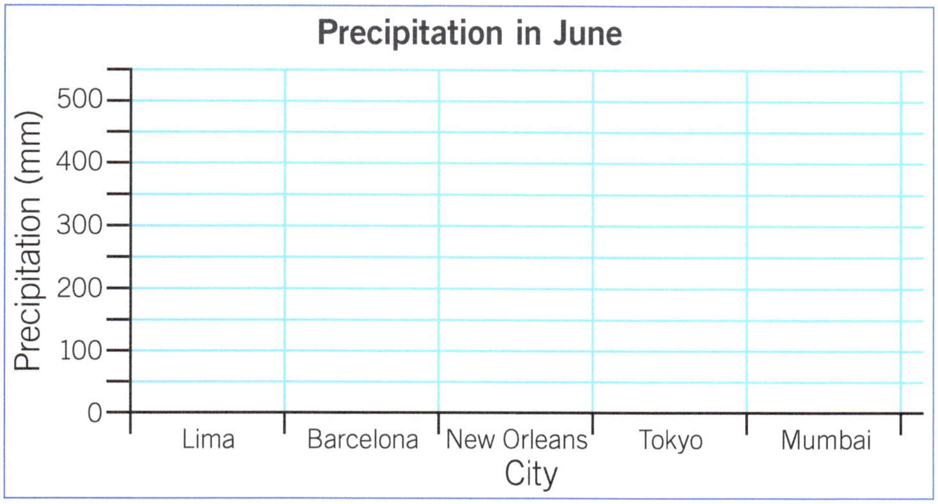

Let's Summarize

An instrument that measures precipitation is called a ______________________.
(pluviometer / anemometer)

Quiz Yourself

1. What instruments would you use to measure the weather characteristics in this environment? Explain what information you would look for.

____

____

____

____

____

____

Research Question

How Can We Measure the Temperature of the Classroom?

What Do I Need?

- a thermometer

What Do I Do?

1. Your teacher will put the thermometer on the wall of the classroom where everyone can see it.
2. In groups, observe the changes in temperature of your classroom. Record the temperature at the same time every day for one week.
3. Record the weather each day as sunny, partly sunny, cloudy or rainy.

To measure is to collect information using instruments.

To communicate is to share written or spoken information with others.

Results

1. Write your observations in the table.

Date / Time	Temperature (°C)	Weather
Monday _______ at __________		
Tuesday _______ at __________		
Wednesday _______ at _______		
Thursday _______ at _________		
Friday _______ at ___________		

Conclusion

1. Complete the text to record your results.

Classroom Temperature

- We measured the temperature from Monday ________________ to Friday ________________.
- Every day the temperature was measured at ________________.
- In general, during the week the weather was ________________.
- The lowest temperature was ________________ °C.
- The highest temperature was ________________ °C.
- Our classroom temperature is ____.

2. Present your group's results to the class. Make a graph of the temperatures or a diagram of the weather.

3. Compare the measurements of each group. Are they similar or different?

In this science lab, you **measured** temperature using the correct instrument. Then you organized the results of your investigation and **communicated** the information to others.

In science, it is important to communicate information in a clear and organized way.

Let's Check!

1. Write the weather characteristics in each picture.

2. How does the weather change between summer and winter in your country? Mark the correct answer with a ✔.

A The temperature and precipitation increase.

B The temperature decreases and precipitation increases.

C The temperature increases and precipitation decreases.

3. What season does the picture show? Explain your answer using the weather characteristics in the picture.

4. Write the number of each weather characteristic next to the correct instrument.

① wind speed ② temperature ③ precipitation ④ wind direction

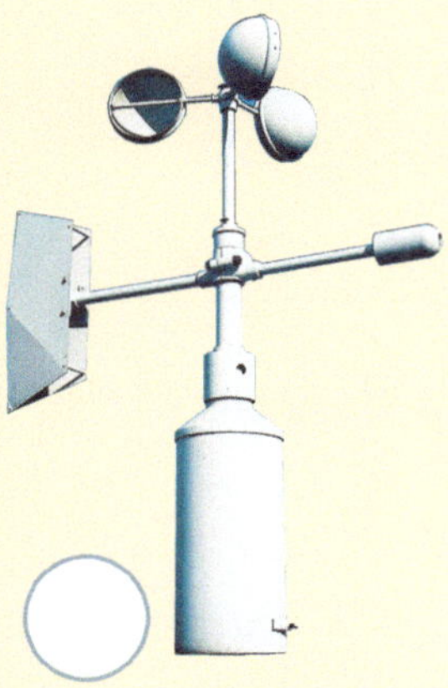

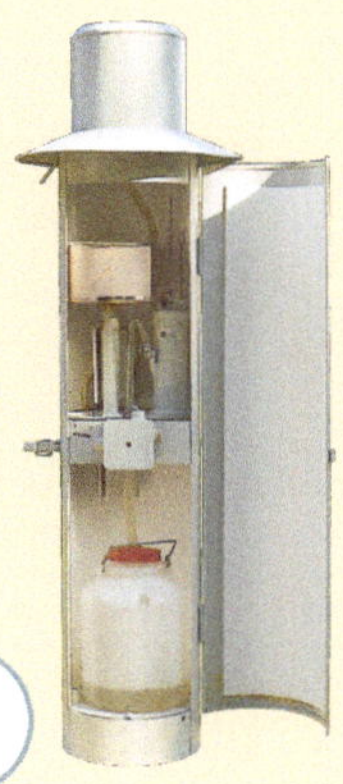

thermometer weather vane anemometer pluviometer

How Did You Do?

For each ☺ color a ⬭.

Effects on Animals

Let's Connect

1. Animals adapt to weather changes during the year. Look at how some animals adapt to the winter. Answer the questions. Analyze

Some animals **hibernate**. They go into a deep sleep for days, weeks or even months, staying in their caves or burrows all winter. By not moving, they conserve body heat. Examples of animals that hibernate are **hedgehogs**, **bears** and **bats**.

Other animals **migrate**. They move to warmer places during the winter. Examples of animals that migrate are **swallows**, **storks**, **monarch butterflies**, some species of **fish** and marine mammals like **whales** and **seals**.

a. Why do animals **hibernate** or **migrate** in the winter but **not in the summer**?

____

b. Think about your pet or another **domestic animal**. Do pets **change** their behavior when the temperature **decreases**? Describe

____

Weather changes, like the colder temperatures, and lack of food in the winter cause some animals to hibernate or migrate.

Fun Fact!

Groundhog Day is celebrated on February 2. It is said that if a groundhog comes out of hibernation and sees its shadow, there will be six more weeks of winter.

Let's Practice

2. If the animal **hibernates**, write an **H**. If the animal **migrates**, write an **M**. Identify

3. **Terrestrial turtles (those that live on land)** hibernate during cold weather. How do you think their **bodies** protect them from cold temperatures? Infer

When the temperature is high, animals can cool their bodies in different ways. For example, a dog **pants** and an elephant covers itself in mud to lower their internal temperatures. What do you do when it is hot?

Let's Summarize

Explain what each word means for animals in the winter.

- **Hibernate:**
- **Migrate:**

Effects on Plants

Let's Connect

1. Look at the pictures. Describe two differences between the pictures. Contrast

differences

____

____

Plants are also affected by the weather. Some trees **lose their leaves** in the fall and grow them back in the spring. Examples are the oak, maple, beech, willow and poplar.

Other trees **keep their leaves** all year, like the eucalyptus, pine, fir, cypress and cedar.

Most plants **flower in the spring** and **produce fruit in the summer**.

Did You Know...?

Parks usually have trees that lose their leaves in the fall and trees that keep them. If you observe a park over a year, you will see many changes!

Let's Practice

2. Circle the trees that **lose** their leaves in the fall in [brown]. Circle the trees that keep their leaves all year in [green]. Identify

3. Go to **Sticker Set 9** on **page 157**. Stick the trees under the correct seasons. Sequence

spring	summer	fall	winter

Let's Summarize

Weather changes have an ______________________ on plants. Some trees lose their leaves in the ______________________. Most trees flower in the ______________________ and produce fruit in the ______________________.

Effects on Humans

Let's Connect

1. Look at the pictures of outdoor activities. Mark the correct answers. Identify

◯ These activities are for **sunny** days.

◯ These activities are for **rainy** and **windy** days.

◯ These activities are for **nice** days.

Challenge

Sing "Rain, Rain, Go Away." (Ask your teacher for the music.) Perform it for your class.

It is helpful to know the weather **forecast** because it helps us plan activities, like playing sports or taking boat trips. The weather can also affect certain **economic activities**, like fishing, agriculture, construction and tourism.

Education through Values

When there is rain and wind or the temperature is low, some people in the world become victims of the bad weather. In the worst cases, they can lose their homes because of **flooding** or **hurricanes**. It is important to donate food or clothes to people in need when we can.

Let's Practice

2. What weather characteristics could affect the people in the pictures? Explain. Infer

______________________ ______________________

______________________ ______________________

Let's Summarize

The weather affects human activities, like:

____

Quiz Yourself

1. Describe how animals and plants adapt to this season. Think of how animals and plants lived in the previous season.

cherry blossom

animals ▸ ______________________

____

____

plants ▸ ______________________

____

____

What Did You Learn?

Mark the correct answers with a ✓.

1. The temperature, precipitation and wind are all:

   A characteristics of weather.

   B instruments to measure weather.

   C characteristics of the seasons.

2. In the winter, some animals save energy by resting. What is this called?

   A Migration.

   B Hibernation.

   C Precipitation.

3. Describe the weather characteristics in the picture.

4. Write **T** for true and **F** for false.

a. ______ To measure temperature, I use a thermometer.

b. ______ To measure wind direction, I use an anemometer.

c. ______ To measure precipitation, I use a pluviometer.

d. ______ To measure wind direction, I use a weather vane.

e. ______ The direction and speed of the wind can be measured with the same instrument.

Scientific Skill: Communicate

5. The table shows the precipitation and temperature on one day in December in two North American cities. Complete the information.

Weather in Vancouver and Houston, December

	Vancouver	Houston
Precipitation (mm)	6	3
Temperature (°C)	6	18

title of table ▶ ____________________

measurements used ▶ ____________________

place(s) ▶ ____________________

measurement results ▶ ____________________

How Did You Do?

For each ☺ color a ⬭.

Invertebrate Album

Go to **Cutout 3** on **page 143**. Learn about more groups of invertebrates. Complete the album.

Mollusks Their bodies are soft, and they do not have different segments. Many have shells to protect them.	clam	snail
Coelenterates These live only in water, and they have one or two tentacles close to their mouths.	jellyfish	coral
Echinoderms These live in the ocean, and their bodies are made of hard plates and spines.	sea urchin	starfish
Annelids These have bodies that are segmented in rings.	earthworm	leech

Glossary

2.1 Key Words Unit 1

breathe – *v*, to take air into your lungs and then expel it

habitat – *n*, the place where a plant or animal naturally lives

hatch – *v*, to come out of an egg; to be born from an egg

move – *v*, to change the location of your body or body parts

respect – *v*, to treat something in a proper way

2.2 Key Words Unit 2

clean – *adj*, not dirty or contaminated

garbage – *n*, trash, unwanted items

hunt – *v*, to chase and kill animals for food or sport

risk – *n*, danger; the chance of something bad happening

shelter – *n*, a structure or place that protects people or animals

2.3 Key Words Unit 3

exercise – *n*, physical activity that is done in order to make your body healthy

measure – *v*, to find out the size, length or amount of something

plan – *n*, a drawing that shows details of a town or building

protect – *v*, to keep safe from harm or danger

pump – *v*, to push liquid from one place to another

2.4 Key Words Unit 4

container – *n*, an object that holds other objects or liquids

faucet – *n*, a tap from which water flows

liquid – *n*, a substance that can flow and conforms easily to other shapes

pollution – *n*, contamination of the environment by foreign substances

temperature – *n*, a measurement of how hot or cold the air or an object is

2.5 Key Words Unit 5

communicate – *v*, to exchange information and ideas through writing, speaking or other methods

environment – *n*, the natural world; the conditions that surround us

season – *n*, one of the four periods of the year characterized by different weather and temperature

storm – *n*, bad weather with lots of rain, snow and/or wind

A

abandon – *v*, to leave, desert or get rid of something

adapt – *v*, to change according to the surroundings

air – *n*, the invisible mix of gases that we breathe

aquarium – *n*, a small tank of water where aquatic animals and plants live

atmosphere – *n*, all the air that surrounds the earth

B

branch – *n*, a part of a tree that grows from the trunk and usually has leaves

C

climate – *n*, the temperature and weather characteristics of an area

consequence – *n*, the result of an action

conservation – *n*, protection or careful use of something

contract – *v*, to reduce in size, get smaller

cycle – *n*, a repeating series of events

D

decide – *v*, to make a choice or decision

decrease – *v*, to become lesser or smaller in quantity or size

deforestation – *n*, the cutting down or burning of all the trees in an area

develop – *v*, to grow, expand or advance

digestion – *n*, the process of food mixing and changing in the body

dissolve – *v*, to mix a solid with a liquid to form a solution

diurnal – *adj*, active during the day

E

economic – *adj*, related to the economy, money and trade

exhale – *v*, to breathe air out of your body

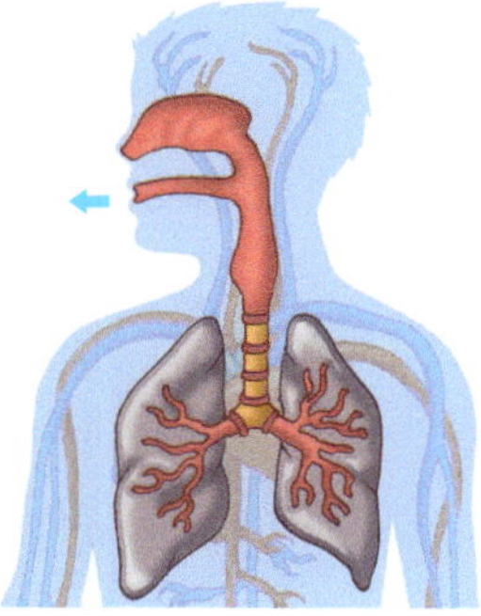

exhausted – *adj*, very tired

expand – *v*, to become bigger

F

flood – *v*, to fill or cover with a large amount of water

forecast – *n*, a prediction or an estimate of the weather

G

garden – *n*, land near a house used for growing plants like flowers or vegetables

global warming – *n*, the increase in temperature of the entire planet

H

hail – *n*, pieces of ice that fall from clouds like rain

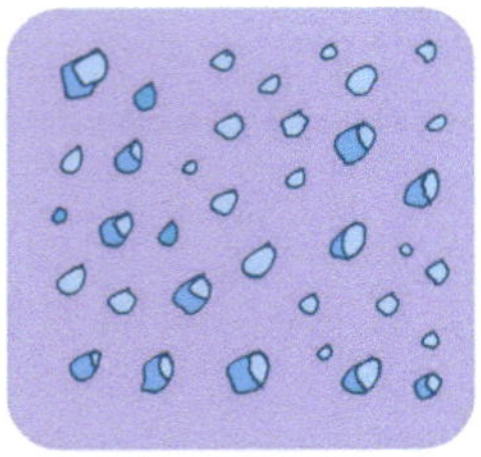

helmet – *n*

I

increase – *v*, to become greater or larger in quantity or size

inhale – *v*, to breathe air in through your mouth and nose

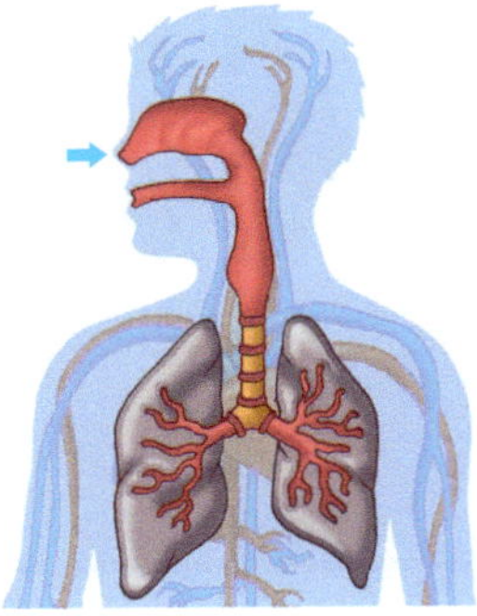

L

lifestyle – *n*, a way of life; habits and routines

M

migrate – *v*, to change location each season

milk – *n*, a white liquid produced by female mammals to feed their young

moderate – *adj*, average, not too much or too little

N

nocturnal – *adj*, active during the night

O

occupy – *v*, to take up space

offspring – *n*, the young of animals or people

oil spill – *n*, the contamination of water with petroleum

organ – *n*, a part of the body that has a specific function

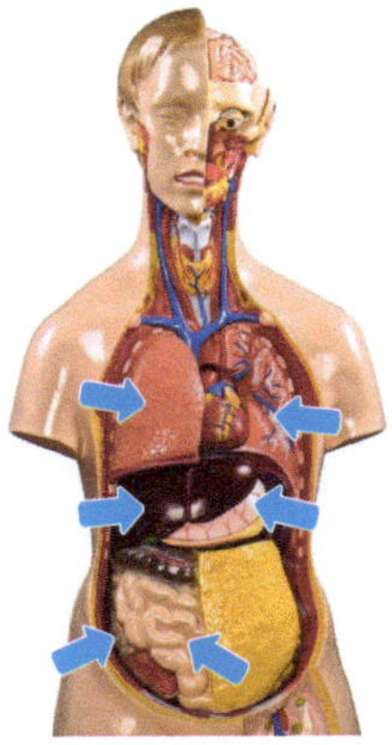

overexposure – *n*, too much contact with a substance or thing without protection

P

precaution – *n*, an action taken to prevent something bad from happening

precipitation – *n*, water that falls from the sky as rain, snow or hail

R

rainfall – *n*, rain or precipitation; the amount of rain in a certain area

respiration – *n*, the action of breathing

rise – *v*, to move upward

rotate – *v*, to turn in a circle

S

skeleton – *n*, the bone structure that supports the body

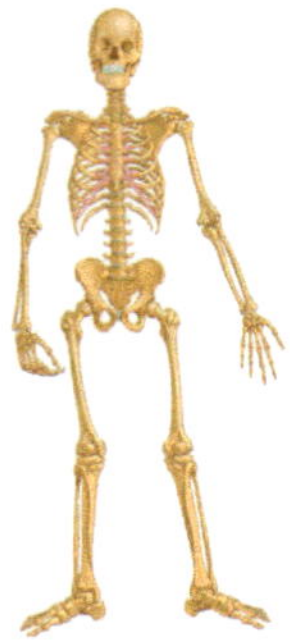

strengthen – *v*, to become stronger

stretch – *v*, to extend a muscle or the body to its full length

sunblock – *n*, lotion that protects your skin from the sun

sunburn – *n*, when skin becomes painful and red from being in the sun

T

temperature – *n*, a measure of how hot or cold something is

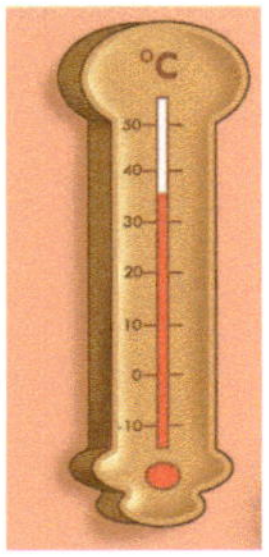

thirsty – *adj*, when you feel like drinking water

tilt – *v*, to place at an angle

tissue – *n*, soft paper used to blow the nose or clean the hands

V

vital – *adj*, important, necessary or essential

W

womb – *n*, the female organ where mammalian offspring develop

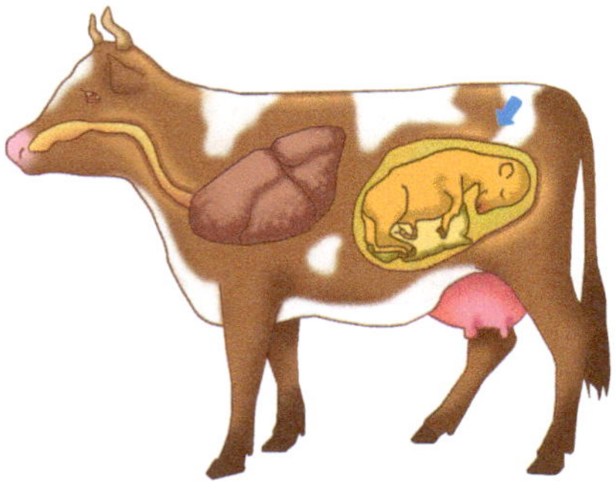

Cutout 1

Use on page 21 (**Unit 1**).

D.R. © Richmond Publishing, S.A. de C.V., 2014

Cutout 2

Use on page 34 (**Unit 1**).

D.R. © Richmond Publishing, S.A. de C.V., 2014

Cutout 3

Use on page 132 (**Invertebrate Album**).

D.R. © Richmond Publishing, S.A. de C.V., 2014

Cutout 4

Use on page 43 (**Unit 2**).

D.R. © Richmond Publishing, S.A. de C.V., 2014

Cutout 5

Use on page 73 (**Unit 3**).

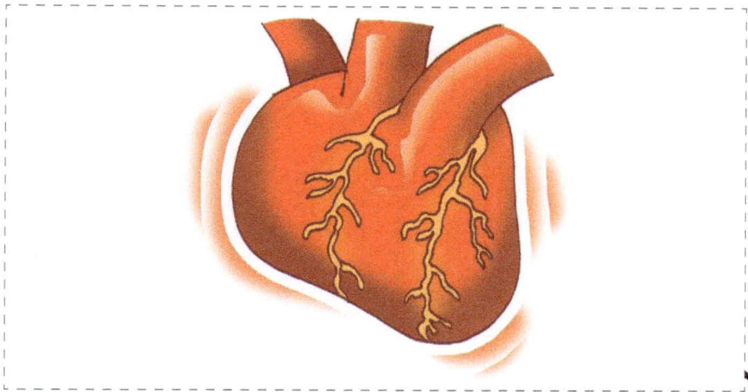

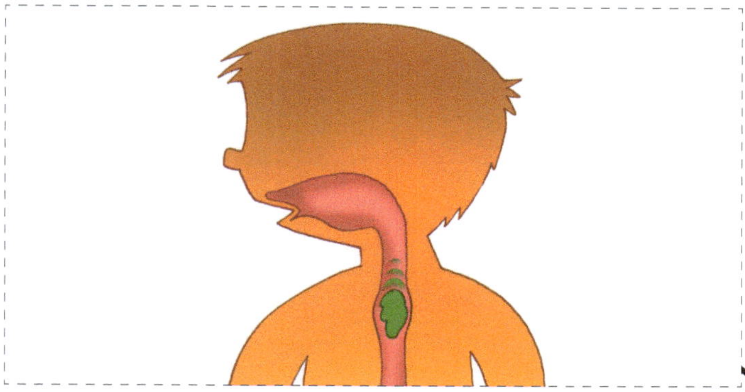

Cutout 6

Use on page 93 (**Unit 4**).

D.R. © Richmond Publishing, S.A. de C.V., 2014

Cutout 7

Use on page 112 (**Unit 5**).

D.R. © Richmond Publishing, S.A. de C.V., 2014

Sticker Set 1
Use on page 19 (**Unit 1**).

Sticker Set 2
Use on page 30 (**Unit 1**).

Sticker Set 3
Use on page 35 (**Unit 1**).

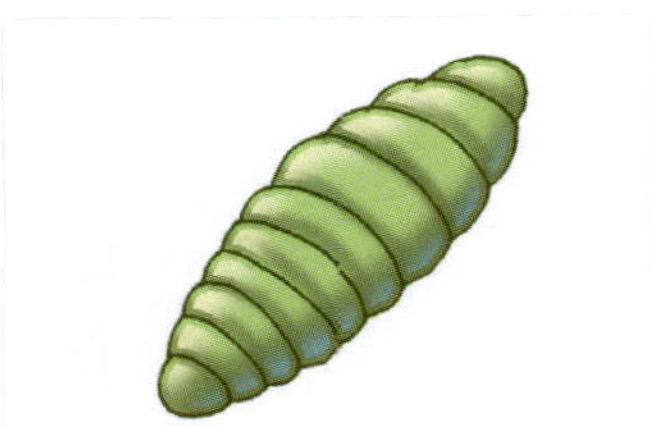

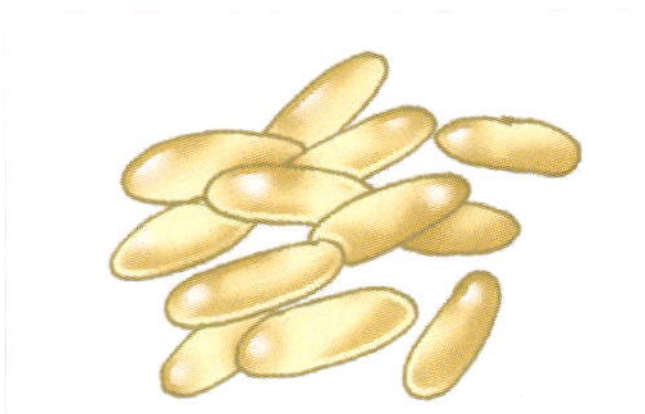

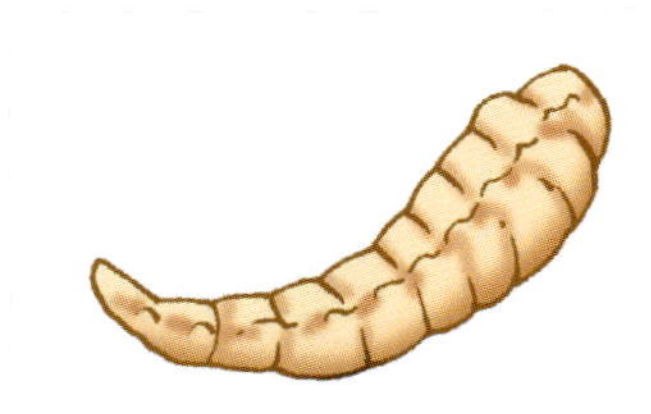

D.R. © Richmond Publishing, S.A. de C.V., 2014

Sticker Set 4

Use on page 39 (**Unit 2**).

Sticker Set 5

Use on page 49 (**Unit 2**).

D.R. © Richmond Publishing, S.A. de C.V., 2014

Sticker Set 6

Use on page 61 (**Unit 3**).

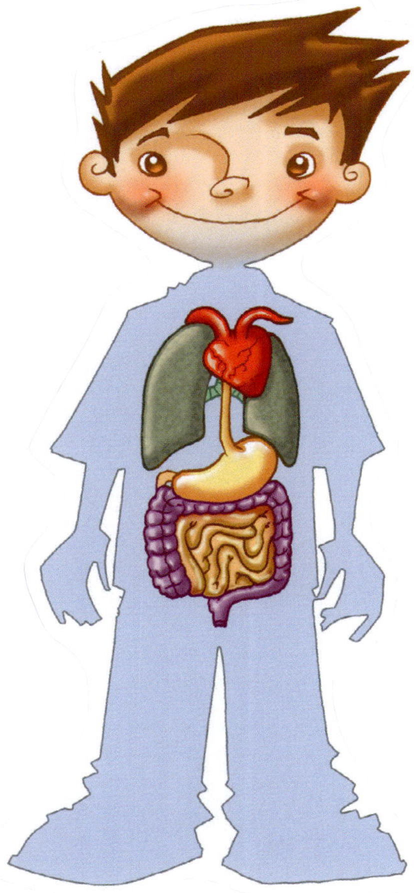

Sticker Set 7

Use on page 85 (**Unit 4**).

D.R. © Richmond Publishing, S.A. de C.V., 2014

Sticker Set 6

Use on page 61 (**Unit 3**).

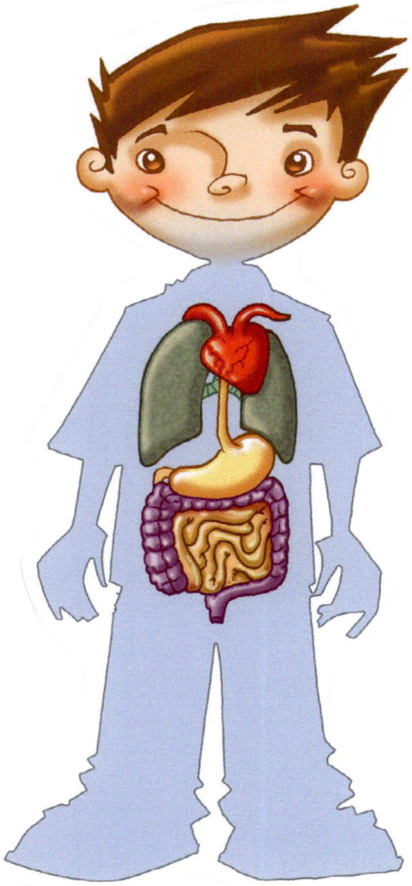

Sticker Set 7

Use on page 85 (**Unit 4**).

D.R. © Richmond Publishing, S.A. de C.V., 2014

Name: ______________________ Grade: __________

Weather Instruments

Temperature

Thermometer

Wind Direction

Weather Vane

Wind Speed

Anemometer

Precipitation

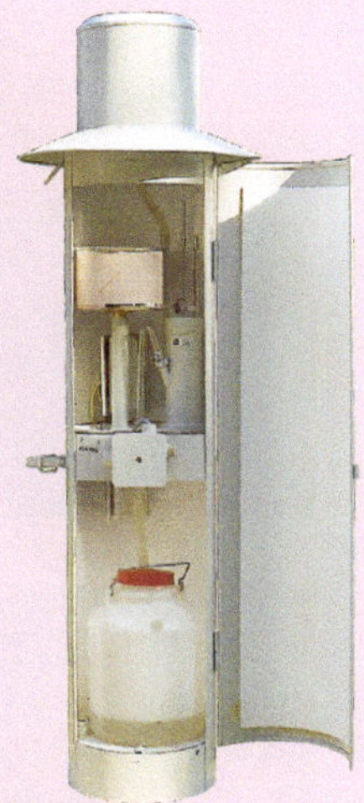

Pluviometer

- Plants and animals have different ways of adapting to weather changes.
- Animals hibernate (stay in a state of rest) or migrate (move to another place) during the cold winter months.
- Some trees and bushes lose their leaves in the fall, and others keep them all year long.
- Humans change their clothing and activities as the weather changes.

Test 5 Study Page • Review

Remove, answer, and glue in your notebook.

Section 1

1. Write the weather characteristics you see in the pictures.

Pathway to Science D.R. © Richmond Publishing, S.A. de C.V., 2014

Section 2

2. How would you use scientific instruments to measure the weather characteristics in the picture? Explain.

____

____

____

____

Section 3

3. Which of these things happen in the spring? Mark the correct answers.

- ◯ Animals hibernate.
- ◯ Animals return home after migrating.
- ◯ Plants grow.
- ◯ People prefer to play inside.
- ◯ Trees lose their leaves.
- ◯ We wear less clothing.

glue here

glue here

glue here

glue here

glue here

Test 5 Study Page • Summary

Weather Characteristics

Temperature: the measurement related to hot and cold either in the environment or in a body. When the temperature is low, it is cold, and when it is high, it is warm or hot.

Wind: the stream of air that comes from the atmosphere.

Precipitation: water that falls from clouds in the form of rain, hail or snow.

Weather changes during the year depending on the season.

Pathway to Science D.R. © Richmond Publishing, S.A. de C.V., 2014

Name: ______________________________ Grade: ____________

When water is exposed to different temperatures, its physical state changes.

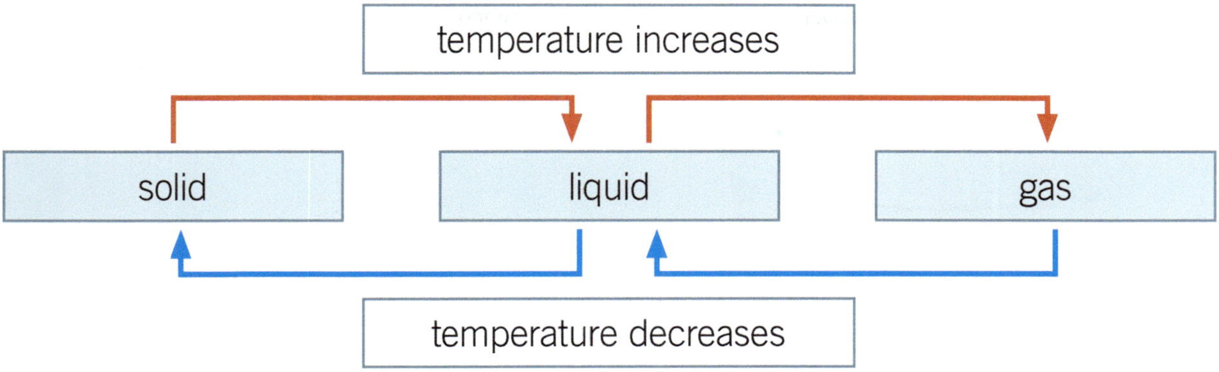

Water is everywhere in nature. It can be found as snow, hail, rain, vapor and in liquid form in rivers, lakes and oceans. These are all parts of the water cycle.

There is very little fresh water on earth, and some of it is polluted by humans through domestic, industrial and agricultural activities. This is why it is important not to waste water and to keep it clean.

Test 4 Study Page • Review

Remove, answer, and glue in your notebook.

Section 1

1. Look at the glass of water. Describe its properties.

____

____

____

____

Section 2

2. Complete each sentence with the correct word.

ice – vapor – liquid – increases – solid – decreases

Water that boils in a kettle, becomes ______________________________.

If you put water in the freezer, it becomes ______________________________.

When the temperature ______________, ice melts and becomes liquid again.

Water in ______________________ form has a defined shape.

Pathway to Science D.R. © Richmond Publishing, S.A. de C.V., 2014

Section 3

3. Number the stages of the water cycle in order.

- [ ] Ice, snow and hail melt and become liquid again, returning to bodies of water like oceans and rivers.
- [ ] Water soaks into the ground.
- [ ] Water evaporates because of increases in temperature.
- [ ] Water vapor condenses to form clouds.

4. Mark the pictures where water is being protected and conserved with a ✓.

Water

Water is very important for all living things on earth. It has the following properties:

- It is odorless: it has no smell.
- It is colorless: it has no color.
- It is transparent: you can see through it.
- It is tasteless: it has no taste.
- It flows.
- It drains.
- It adapts to the shape of the container it is in.
- It dissolves some solids, like sugar and salt.

Water has three physical states:

Physical State	Example	Property
solid	ice	It has a defined shape.
liquid	rain	It adapts to the shape of the container it is in.
gas	vapor	It occupies available space.

Pathway to Science D.R. © Richmond Publishing, S.A. de C.V., 2014

Name: ______________________ Grade: __________

Exercise

Exercise develops muscles and strengthens the heart. You should play sports or ride a bike to stay healthy!

Eating well and spending less time watching TV or on the computer also makes you healthier.

Test 3 Study Page • Review

Remove, complete, and glue in your notebook.

Section 1

1. Draw the heart, lungs and stomach. Write their functions.

- heart ▶ ______________________
- lungs ▶ ______________________
- stomach ▶ ______________________

Section 2

2. Explain the function of muscles and bones in the body.

____

____

Pathway to Science D.R. © Richmond Publishing, S.A. de C.V., 2014

Section 3

3. Mark which pictures have positive effects on the heart and muscles.

a. Why are these actions good for your health? Explain.

____

____

____

glue here

glue here

glue here

glue here

glue here

Human Organs

The **lungs** are two organs that allow us to breathe and use the oxygen in the air.

The **heart** pumps blood to all body parts.

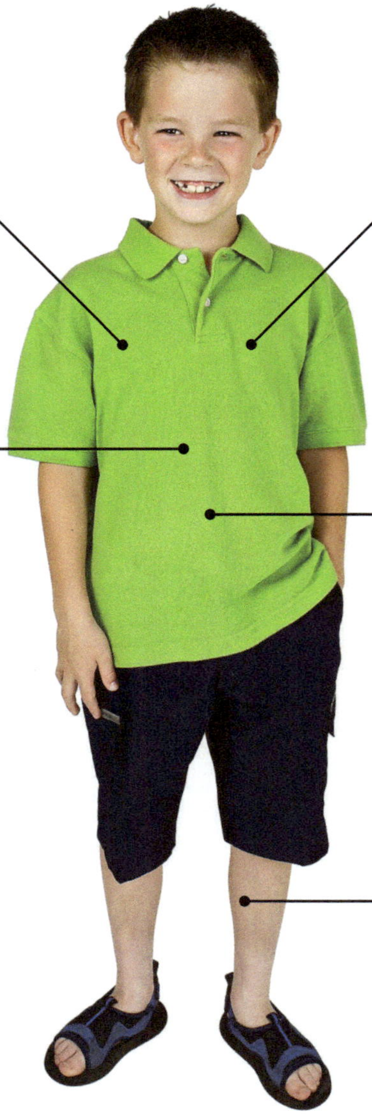

The **skeleton** supports and gives shape to the body. It protects vital organs and has bones connected by joints.

The **stomach** mixes and transforms food before it goes to the intestines.

Muscles are a kind of tissue that contracts and expands. With the help of bones, they allow us to move.

Pathway to Science D.R. © Richmond Publishing, S.A. de C.V., 2014

Name: ______________________________ Grade: __________

Human activity affects the environment. The impact can be positive or negative.

Negative Impacts	Positive Impacts
• Wasting water and electricity. • Hunting endangered animals or hunting many animals. • Polluting the air or water, or littering. • Cutting down trees in the forest. • Causing forest fires.	• Creating protected areas for plants and animals. • Controlling the use of water and energy. • Planting trees, picking up garbage and preventing forest fires. • Using the Three Rs (Reduce, Reuse and Recycle).

Endangered Native Animals

Animals that are originally from the place they live are called native animals. Some native animals at risk of extinction are:

giant panda

Bengal tiger

California condor

bison

red wolf

parakeet

blue whale

Test 2 Study Page • Review

Remove, answer, and glue in your notebook.

Section 1

1. Mark the correct habitat for the animal shown.

- ocean
- desert

a. What is the turtle's habitat like?

light ▶ ______________________________

____

____

humidity ▶ ______________________________

____

____

warm or cold ▶ ______________________________

____

____

Pathway to Science D.R. © Richmond Publishing, S.A. de C.V., 2014

Section 2

2. Match the human activities that have negative impacts on the environment with their solutions.

Letting the water run while you brush your teeth.	Ride a bicycle instead of using a car.
Cutting down trees to build houses.	Plant trees and bushes in open spaces.
Going camping and leaving garbage in the forest.	Throw away garbage in appropriate places.
Using a car in the city.	Use a cup of water to brush your teeth.

Section 3

3. What human behaviors have caused animals to lose their habitats and be put at risk of extinction? How are animals affected when they lose their habitats because of negative human actions?

____

____

____

glue here

glue here

glue here

glue here

glue here

Habitat

The place where animals live is called their habitat. Habitats can be forests, deserts, oceans or wherever animals live. Different animals live in each habitat.

Habitat Characteristics

Light affects animal life in different habitats. Some animals are awake during the day (diurnal), and others are awake at night (nocturnal).

Temperature affects animals' bodies and behavior. Every animal lives in a habitat where the temperature is right for it.

Humidity is the amount of water in a habitat. Water is very important for animals, and some even live in it.

Pathway to Science D.R. © Richmond Publishing, S.A. de C.V., 2014

Name: ______________________ Grade: __________

- Invertebrates are classified in different groups. The biggest group is arthropods.

Arthropods
• Their body is divided into three parts: head, thorax and abdomen. **Insects** have two antennae and six legs. **Arachnids** have eight legs. **Crustaceans** have four antennae and ten legs. Many crustaceans have a hard shell for protection.

- All living beings have a life cycle, and some go through a process of metamorphosis.

Test 1 Study Page • Review

Remove, answer, and glue in your notebook.

Section 1

1. Complete the table comparing the groups of animals.

Mammals	Characteristics	Birds
	body covering	
	respiration	
	number and type of limbs	
	how they reproduce	
	habitat	

Section 2

2. Color the circles with each animal's characteristics.

oviparous · viviparous · feathers · scales · hairless

lungs · gills · land · water · air

Pathway to Science D.R. © Richmond Publishing, S.A. de C.V., 2014

Section 3

3. Put each arthropod in the correct group.

spider | butterfly | lobster
grasshopper | dragonfly | crab

Insects	Arachnids	Crustaceans

Section 4

4. Draw the missing stages in the butterfly's life cycle.

glue here
glue here
glue here
glue here
glue here

Test 1 Study Page • Summary

Animals

- vertebrates (have a skeleton)
- invertebrates (do not have a skeleton)

- Vertebrates are classified in different groups according to these characteristics:

	Mammals	Birds	Reptiles	Fish	Amphibians
Hair	✓				
Scales			✓	✓	
Feathers		✓			
Hairless					✓
Lungs	✓	✓	✓		✓
Gills				✓	✓
Drink milk	✓				
Viviparous	✓				
Oviparous		✓	✓	✓	✓
Terrestrial	✓	✓	✓		✓
Aquatic	✓	✓	✓	✓	✓
Aerial	✓	✓			

Pathway to Science D.R. © Richmond Publishing, S.A. de C.V., 2014

Sticker Set 8

Use on page 109 (**Unit 5**).

Sticker Set 9

Use on page 127 (**Unit 5**).

D.R. © Richmond Publishing, S.A. de C.V., 2014